D0783164

CHOLOS & SURFERS
A Latino Family Album

CHOLOS
&
SURFERS

A Latino Family Album

Jack López

CAPRA PRESS
SANTA BARBARA

Copyright © 1998 by Jack López
All rights reserved.
Printed in the United States of America.

Cover design and book design by Frank Goad, Santa Barbara

Cover photograph of family used by permission of Agripina Lopez (née Estavillo),
Francis Estavillo (née Padilla) and Pablo Estavillo and children;
cover photograph of surfers used by permission of Ventura County Museum of History and Art

"Of Cholos and Surfers" first appeared in *Muy Macho:
Latino Men Confront Their Manhood*

"Pathos, Bathos, and Mexiphobia" was first published in *The Massachusetts Review*

Special thanks to Julie Popkin, resolute agent, dear friend.

LIBRARY OF CONGRESS CATALOGING-IN-PUBLICATION DATA

López, Jack, 1950–
Cholos and surfers / Jack López
p. cm.
ISBN 0-88496-429-9 (pbk. : alk. paper)
1. López, Jack, 1950– —Childhood and youth. 2. Hispanic Americans—California—Los Angeles—
Biography 3. Los Angeles (Calif.)—Ethnic relations. 4. Los Angeles (Calif.)—Biography.
I. Title.
F869.L89S754 1998
979.4'93053'092—dc21
[B]
97-48564
CIP

CAPRA PRESS
POST OFFICE BOX 2068
SANTA BARBARA, CA 93120

for my father
Robert John Lopez

"Everybody is right from his own standpoint,
but it is not impossible that everybody is wrong."
—MOHANDAS GANDHI

CONTENTS

ORDINARY WISDOM

In **1969** in my first college composition class I wrote a maudlin essay titled "One Man." It was a paean to my older brother whom I loved dearly and whom I had great respect for. He died of AIDS in 1987, and my father and I were at his bedside, I clinging to his leg, wishing him safe travels, knowing he didn't wish to be on this earth any longer—he refused any artificial life support—while my father commanded the doctor to do something, anything, in a high pitched, unnatural, agitated voice.

The doctor couldn't do anything.

When the monitor went flat, my father, the doctor, and I hugged each other next to my newly dead brother. We all cried. My brother's eyes were still open, staring straight up into the ceiling.

My family, of course, never recovered from this. Though we all knew my brother was at risk, we all knew he was gay, we all knew he'd taken heroin, we all knew he'd lived in NYC at the height of the post 60s hedonism, and had lived there into the early 80s, when many artists were dying, still, we thought we were blessed. Things that raw and "life-and-death" wouldn't happen to us. Sure, all the grandparents had died, but this was in the natural order of things, this was expected, they were old. My brother was "young." Had he lived, he would have celebrated his forty-first birthday the month after his deathday.

I had just finished graduate school, and my brother had given me an expensive watch, a wonderful watch, a magnificent watch, a watch I couldn't wear for five years—it was too painful. He was proud of the fact that I had finished graduate school, that I would be teaching. He wanted me to wear the watch when in class. Prior to graduate school I had made money in construction, even though I had an undergraduate degree.

While in graduate school I met the woman who would become my wife; one of the professors who ran the writing program—they only accepted six applicants a year, from a pool of hundreds—brought her in as a visiting writer. She too was a graduate of the program, though she'd finished many years earlier, and had books out, and had a tenure track position at a major writing program in the South. The professor who brought her in as a visiting writer was a surrogate father to her. He told her to stay away from me. I was newly divorced. The service provided, the other professor who ran the program liked to say.

About three weeks before my brother's death my wife and I visited my brother in his apartment in Los Feliz, where he showed us his art, which he was so proud of and which he'd purchased in New York. He presented me my watch while we were in his apartment. He was setting things in order.

We went out to dinner that night, I complained about graduate school stuff, and we drank margaritas. This was really something because my brother had been clean and sober four years prior to his drinking with us that night. He asked me how I felt about it. His drinking. I asked him how did he feel about it. I've been mighty dry, my brother said.

After dinner we went to the movies and saw *Withnail and I*. My brother and my wife howled through the funny movie, and my brother was so pleased I was finally with a woman such as my wife: educated (Vassar), intelligent, witty, beautiful. He was pleased with us both.

Maybe that made him feel celebratory, I don't know. He drank with us that night, after being clean and sober for so long. And he stopped by a friend's apartment in Century City, and left my wife and me sitting in his car for a long time, and I know he scored some junk, because he had that runny-nosed excitement of people who have just shot up.

Celebration or suicide?

I'll never know.

He holed up in his apartment. I knew—my younger brother and I cleaned out his apartment after his death, and I saw the dirty plates of leftover food, which he'd tried in vain to eat, and I saw where he'd been sick in the bathroom, which I also cleaned, and saw a publication of mine, next to his bed. Finally, a friend forced him to enter the hospital.

The day my wife and I were going to move in together. The day I showed up at my parents' house to borrow boxes for the move; the day I heard my mother shrieking and I thought my father'd had a heart attack since he was the one who'd had open heart surgery and we thought he was next on God's list. He wasn't, however. My brother was. A doctor had called my mother and father. The doctor told them to get to the hospital as soon as possible. My brother was dying. The doctor didn't want my brother to die alone, even though my brother didn't wish to involve us. The stigma associated with AIDS was far greater in 1987 than now, though there's still shame associated with it in some people's minds.

My mother and younger brother had gone out to get a breath of fresh air, when my older brother left the ether. My sister had gone home with her husband—it was around two in the morning and we'd been there all day. At Cedars Sinai Hospital in West Los Angeles. Across the street from the Beverly Center. A hospital administrator had given us a room, sort of like an apartment living room. They thought we'd be there for a while. They said sometimes the patients rally with the appearance of the family. After my brother's death my mother, my father, my younger brother and I prayed in the room. Then we gathered my brother's effects and drove home on the empty Los Angeles freeways. Beaten and alone on an early August morning.

♦

My family stayed together a lot in those days following my brother's death: we celebrated his life; we told stories; we cried; we raged; we laughed; we fought. We were still a family, though we'd lost a member, and the numbers would never again be right—five instead of six.

Parents aren't supposed to bury their children. Unfortunately this happens all the time. We feel that this is out of the natural order, unnatural. And I can't conceive the pain and loss my parents endured, still endure, with the death of their son. The eldest. I know the depths of grief I suffered as a sibling.

My parents and I have always been close. After my brother's death we developed a series of new rituals to deal with our grief. One such ritual was getting sandwiches at Gallo's in Corona del Mar and then picnicking by the beach. We talked a lot those afternoons, talked and cried and remembered my brother, for you must remember the dead, you must, even though everyone else would just as soon forget.

My mother was inconsolable for a number of years, and my father was raw too, though he was strong for my mother, taking up the slack around the house, taking up the slack emotionally.

♦

Before our marriage my soon-to-be wife and I would live together. She'd asked me point blank what my intentions were, did I envision us together? I did, I loved her very much, which certainly wasn't enough, I know now, but I'd never been with anyone who was so clear about how to make a relationship work. And work it is. As my parents know. My father always told me that his marriage was a partnership. It seemed to be so now, now that they were older, for in his younger days my father couldn't have been that easy to live with.

So we moved on, my family and I. I was formally married again, my younger brother was married as well, my sister and her husband moved to Los Gatos for their careers. My wife got a job at a different school, and we moved about an hour's drive from my parents. Life stabilized somewhat, and we tried to work through our grief, and time does take much of the sting out of those horrible wounds.

Still, we moved forward, we had no choice.

My father'd had open-heart surgery in 1976. We'd been on subconscious deathwatch all that time, I suppose, and we felt tricked, somehow, when my brother died. We weren't ready for that. Since my father's open-heart surgery he's had a series of minor heart attacks, numerous episodes of angina, times when he can't breathe and must take a nitroglycerin tablet. I'm always amazed at his grace, when under these stressful and frightening conditions, he calmly gets out his pill and takes it. Sort of like the grace my brother exhibited before his death.

◆

My parents celebrated their fiftieth wedding anniversary a few years back. My wife was pregnant at the time, and there was much discussion about postponing the celebration of the anniversary to the spring when my wife and new child would be able to attend. I was adamantly opposed to postponing the celebration of the anniversary.

I'd wanted to spend a bunch of money, go into debt even, to celebrate it right. One sibling had no money and the other wasn't willing to go into debt, so we had the party at my parents' house, had it catered, and everyone pitched in. The reason my wife couldn't attend was that she was going to give birth by cesarean on the day before New Year's Eve. My parents had eloped fifty years previous on a New Year's Eve. We celebrated their elopement the Saturday night before New Year's Eve.

I gave the toast at the gathering, and I don't remember it verbatim, but I talked about family and about our larger human tribe, and about a continuum, and about the new family member we would have the following day. And we did. December 30th, my son was born. And we named him for my brother who'd died. While giving the toast at my parents' fiftieth wedding anniversary, before our friends and family members, with my mother and father standing next to me, my brother and sister standing next to them, my father gave me the most beatific look. It was the look of pride and acceptance and approval, and more, it was primal, and we were around the first fire, and we knew we were humans, evolving, moving forward like ants in Uncle Milton's ant farm. I'll never get another look such as that one, I don't think, and that's okay, for if you get only one of those looks in a lifetime, that's just right.

My father has always been supportive of the things I've wanted to do. He guided me, I know, and he cajoled me and yelled at me and cared for me. He took off work early to see me play my games when I was in high school and played right after school. He was so much looking forward to watching me play varsity, on Friday nights under the lights, everything we'd worked for all those years would culminate with his beaming approval from the stands. Except at spring workouts I sprained my ankle, and the head coach threw a football at me as I lay injured on the grass, and I never played organized sports again after that. No matter how many times the coaches came to my classrooms to take me out of class to talk with me. Cursed and abused for getting an injury. I wouldn't be a part of any such system. I didn't tell my father the reason I'd quit football. I suffered his disappointment in silence, for I was an uncommunicative adolescent. But I know this: the reason I quit in the first place, and stuck to my guns, was because of what my father had taught me—you don't take abuse from anyone, never!

The irony is that had I told my father, he would have gone down to the school and given the boorish coach a piece of his mind.

That was how my father was. You didn't let things slide. Especially if injustice was involved. And he disciplined me and my brothers, no matter how much he didn't wish to. You got an appropriate punishment for the crime. No getting out of it.

And he was like this too: Once when a frog got trapped in the dryer duct and "fried" from the heat, my father installed a grate so that no more frogs would die, even though they kept us awake at night with all their croaking. And when after his open-heart surgery he was released from the hospital, even though he could barely walk, he insisted on opening the car door for my mother.

I see now that he went without so that we might have the things we wanted. We weren't poor, just lower middle-class, working class. He was an hourly printer by trade most of his career. He bought beer in the quart bottle since it was cheaper, even though he had a taste for expensive wine. He had a good voice and was musically inclined, and they say he might have been able to make a living as a singer, though he was a mechanic, working with his hands to provide for his family—the same hands that played the violin so skillfully.

My father walked with me on summer evenings when he

wasn't at work, talking about my studies, my sports, my state of being. He walked with me and bought me ice cream. He walked with me and taught me things on those evenings, things I wouldn't learn in school.

When we moved to Huntington Beach and one of my brother's friends came to visit from the old neighborhood, I got so homesick and lonely that my father took me all the way down to the See's Candies shop in Corona del Mar to buy candy to make me feel better. And when I came home with a fat lip and a broken nose he calmly asked me if I wished to take karate lessons. When he and my mother and my little sister and brother returned home from the movies early, and I was in bed with my high school girlfriend, he told me the next day to use protection, for her sake as well as mine. He told me that what I was doing was natural, though not very wise, and if I continued, use protection (in those days the protection was for the sake of not having a child). In another lifetime when I was a child and threw a sparkler on the neighbor's roof and wasn't sure whether or not it was out, I called upon my father. Without hesitation he took me to the neighbor's house, where we three hosed down the roof. Both men praised me for doing the right thing. But I knew what the right thing was from my father's discipline, from his time spent walking and talking with me. Sure, I transgressed, but even at an early age I knew the difference between right and wrong. I wasn't born knowing this, I was taught, mostly by my father.

♦

Once again I'm grieving. A month after my son's birth,

my father suffered an acute stroke. He lost most of his speech, and is now confined to a wheelchair, which he can only exit from with help, and he can't go to the bathroom on his own. My son's birth and my father's stroke are forever entwined in my memory. An extremely joyful event was immediately counterbalanced by a difficult and sad one. As I realized the depth of my father's demise, I also knew that I wished to preserve for my son my father's essence, his core, what he stood for, since my child would be unable to receive this directly from his grandfather. My son will only know his grandfather through the words in this book.

My father was born and raised in Boyle Heights in East Los Angeles. He grew up surrounded not only by Mexican Americans, but also by recently arrived Jews fleeing anti-Semitism, by immigrant White Russians fleeing communism, by newly arrived Asians fleeing persecution. As a teen at the beginning of World War II, he had a job—his father, my grandfather, worked for Union Pacific right through the depression—overseeing and helping thousands of African Americans who arrived in Los Angeles from the South to work the factories during wartime. As a result of his experiences, he taught me not so much a tolerance for other cultures, because tolerance implies endurance or pain, but an excitement to experience the world through the eyes of those who had lived elsewhere, a cultural yearning and awareness, if you will. He also taught me right from wrong.

I've thought a lot about my own youth in Los Angeles in the 1950s, and know that rightly and obviously this time is gone forever. My son's experiences in the 1990s will be radically different from those experienced by me in the 1950s. Change is the way of the universe, and I accept this. But I wish for my son to know my father in a way that is no longer possible—my father's not the same person, post-stroke. So this is why I write—to remember. To formalize my father's sensibility for me, and for my son. And for others, should they desire to know my father, to know of our lives.

HOW WE LIVED

W E DIDN'T TALK about cultural diversity in those days, we lived it in the melting pot our teachers at elementary school spoke of so proudly. I was eight years old. It was 1958 in Los Angeles. The neighbors had these kinds of names: Medina, Brennan, Silverman, Slogett, Ver Haven, Muelich, Johnson. Our ancestors came from Mexico, Spain, Ireland, Israel, England, Dutch Indonesia, Germany, and Africa. Everyone knew these things, but we didn't dwell on them because we knew we were all Americans, even though we had our own unique cultural backgrounds. Besides, as a child, I was too busy learning the hard business of right versus wrong.

And it was during my eighth year, the year I had a paper route, the year Jack H stole my paper money, when I began to realize there were certain people we didn't like, and that our dislike toward them was based upon how they acted, not who they were.

My parents were different, I suppose, in the same way every child views his parents as different, except, since my parents were both raised in Boyle Heights in East Los Angeles, the prevailing expectation was that they would not enter the American mainstream. This wasn't so. I know my father ran track for Roosevelt High School, I've seen the photos. He worked too. And I've been told he had his share of fights, though they were always one on one, no weapons, throwing *chingazos*, in slang. But he also played the violin, and was accomplished enough to perform at the Hollywood Bowl with the Roosevelt High School Senior Orchestra. He hid his violin so the guys wouldn't know he took lessons after school. And I think these are mainstream things, what my father did when a youth in East Los Angeles. He wasn't in a gang, he didn't do time in jail. He was an avid reader, and my mother was too. She had excellent grades, wished to attend college, as did my father, and would have if not for the intrusion of World War II.

Shortly before my father enlisted in the Navy, my parents eloped to Yuma. No large formal Mexican American wedding for them. While my father served in the Pacific, gone for twenty-seven months during the height of hostilities, my mother lived with his parents off Brooklyn Avenue. She saved all my father's Navy allotment checks so they could buy a house. And upon his discharge, my parents built a custom home in Lynwood, where I was born.

I don't remember much from my early childhood. A few sketch-like photo memories: riding on the back window ledge of my father's humongous car; getting haircuts on Tweedy Boulevard; Mr. D, the wheezing grouchy old man who lived across the alley and who had suffered the effects of mustard gas from his war. At the time I was too sick to attend kindergarten. So I sat in front of the picture window in the living room, watching the school kids across the street at play at recess. Then I got better. I entered school in the first grade and did pretty well, for I already knew how to read from all my time spent at home.

There seems to be some pivotal night in the darkness of my memory, and I don't know that I've conveniently linked events for the sake of a narrative. But this is how memory serves us. I was probably in third grade. My older brother came into our room—we shared rooms until his marriage at eighteen—asking if he could borrow a knife. I had a collection, and it wasn't much, though I did have a hunting knife. It seems my brother and his friend Ronny were followed home by some older guys.

I always wondered if Ronny's having my knife escalated that night's violence, or if my knife saved his life. Of course I'll never know the answer to the question. But Ronny was beaten badly enough to land in the hospital. After that, it seems in my memory at least, we moved.

109th Street and Western is on the fringes of Inglewood, Gardena and Watts, but it's Los Angeles. Our house was a three bedroom so my new sister could have her own room. But the first week we lived on 109th Street word spread of an impending gang fight; we'd better keep the streets clear. Fear was palpable, that day my brother and I were kept home from school—my mother knew about the rumor. She tried to keep us indoors, but the allure of the impending fight was far too magnetic a force for my brother and me. We sneaked outside while my mother napped with our baby sister.

We stealthily made our way a few houses up the deserted street, walking next to and in the bushes, not daring to walk across the street. The block remained empty until afternoon, when the workers returned, and everyone felt a sense of safety in numbers. My brother and I saw absolutely

22

nothing happen that gang-fight day, but the intimidation factor had worked successfully on everyone, and my father was furious.

The first time I saw Jack H he loomed over me like some Brobdingnagian urban warrior. The fact that I was in a trench didn't help matters. Washington High School, which was at the end of our block, was having new sewer lines laid and there were land cuts everywhere. The neighborhood kids were playing hide-and-seek. I was hiding. Jack H found me. I looked up out of my burrow into the sun and there he stood, one foot on the mound of dirt at the lip of the trench. His pose was that of a conqueror. He wore scuffed motorcycle boots, dirty Levi's, and a black leather jacket. His blue eyes squinted against a harsh winter's sun, face dispassionate as he stared down at me. His arms were crossed over his chest, crew-cut hair almost golden, but the truly frightening aspect of the encounter, besides the fact that he was a gang leader and much older than I, was the black whip which lay coiled beneath his arm, and upon which his fingers clenched and released, as if they had a mind of their own. We looked at each other for a few seconds until I scurried off on my hands and knees in the dirt.

In those days when you delivered the *Los Angeles Times* on Sunday they gave you a wagon to deliver the papers. Even as a child I worked so I could give good Christmas gifts to my family, or buy sports equipment for myself, or feed my bank account. In autumn, I sold Christmas cards. On Wednesday afternoons I delivered the *Southwest Sun*, a local advertising paper which was deposited at everyone's home, yet only a few kind people would pay the subscription when I collected. But the *Los Angeles Times* was different. People paid or they didn't receive the paper. And I was thrilled to have the Sunday route in our neighborhood. These things don't come easily to a child, because responsibility, integrity and luck all play a part in securing such a job. Lenny M, who lived on the corner and had previously delivered the paper, recommended me to the *Times* man, and I got the route.

The Sunday paper was far too fat for folding and throwing, as was done with the daily paper, thus the high-sided red delivery wagon. On the wood in clean white paint was inscribed *Los Angeles Times*. A feeling of pride enveloped me those early Sunday mornings, placing paper after paper on the neighborhood porches. I'd awaken before five a.m. (with an alarm clock I'd won for selling the most Christmas cards), remove the wagon from the safety of our garage, where it was stored all week, load my first batch of papers—there were three other drop-off points along the route—and begin walking the empty, silent streets. By the end of the route I'd be exhausted, but there was always the big hill on 107th Street where I'd sit in my empty wagon, surfing down the asphalt wave while the neighborhood slept.

Once a month, on Friday afternoon late, I'd collect from my subscribers. I knew that in our house Friday was a good day: payday. And there was a sense of celebration in the air. So I tapped into this prevailing mood in the neighborhood, and it was primarily successful for me, though some people would be out. I'd go back during the week to collect from the few who weren't around.

Since money was involved my older brother accompanied me when collecting. He carried a velour pouch my mother had made to put money in. We'd walk the neighborhood, smelling dinners cooking, hearing people living their lives, and sometimes even saw them in illuminated windows, like tiny fragments from a play, enacted for our enjoyment.

My brother first noticed the black Mercury which seemed to appear and reappear with alarming regularity. I'd seen the car before, though I didn't make the connection until it was too late. So we pressed on, trying to finish the task at hand as afternoon turned to evening. After the last customer's house, my brother and I began our long walk home in a gloomy darkness. As we stepped off a curb to cross the street, the Mercury screeched to a halt in front of us, cutting off our path. Four guys jumped out, Jack H among them. No words were spoken. Jack H made directly for my brother, punched him in the stomach hard, and took from him the velour pouch with my collection money. It all happened so fast. Jack H and his outfit were in their car and speeding away before my brother even had a chance to sit on the walkway grass.

As the black Mercury burned rubber away from us I remembered where I'd seen it before. Washington High School was on Normandie Avenue. Woodcrest Elementary School was east by Vermont. I had to walk past the high school to and from my school. One afternoon on my way home I stood at the stop light at 108th and Normandie. The black Mercury pulled up, Jack H emerged from its smoky bowels, and proceeded to throw blows with a high school boy who was waiting for the bus. He wasn't surprised this seemingly random event was occurring, and I felt he knew Jack H was after him, and that he'd just as soon take his beating and get it over with, which he did.

When the "fight" was finished the black Mercury peeled out burning rubber in its signature departure. The high school kid stood there somewhat dazed with red welts all over his face, and a small trickle of blood rivered over his lip. I helped him pick up his books and told him I wished he'd won. He agreed with me.

Had I been able to identify the Mercury sooner I might have spared my brother the blow he received. But after a time he was okay. We both decided not to tell our parents. We had another lame excuse for not going to the police, though I can no longer recall what it was exactly. We returned home empty-handed, out a month's worth of paper route money, which I replaced from my bank account. But we were much more careful after this experience.

A few months later while walking to the market with my father on a warm spring evening, the Mercury drove past us. It slowed and I became frightened. I imagined Jack H inside, fingering his bullwhip. My father watched the car slow down, not in the least intimidated by its presence. In fact, he shook his head and began laughing. They're just bullies, my father said. They were the ones who tried to crash Ginger's party.

The S family, who lived up the street from us and who were Mexican Americans from Arizona, but who had a coat of arms hanging in their hallway showing their Scots ancestry (all this is another story), had two teenage daughters. Their daughters had a party one Saturday night. My parents helped Phil and Lydia, the other parents, chaperone the party.

Brian S, who was one year younger than I, had told me everything shortly after it happened. The party had gone well, until just after midnight a group of party crashers arrived, forcing their way inside the house. At that point my father and Phil S had said, okay, let's take it outside. Both men were World War II veterans, had seen their share of killing and death. Stepping outside with a bunch of teens, even though outnumbered, probably didn't seem so bad, I suppose. The gist of the story Brian S told me was that not one of those crashers would stand up to my father or his father.

Those were the guys at Ginger's? I repeated. Ginger was the oldest daughter.

That car, my father said. He nodded, all the while keeping his eyes on the Mercury.

I looked up at my father, and saw a slight smile form at the corners of his mouth. He put his arm around me and we quickened our pace. We were, after all, on an ice cream mission for our family. When I looked into the street the car was gone.

It's ironic how I look back on those times, waxing nostalgic for the good old days when a thief punched me in the stomach and stole my money! I've read many articles from the same paper I used to deliver, articles about generations of gang members spawned in East Los Angeles, about the Crips and Bloods in South Central Los Angeles, even the Vietnamese gangs in Orange County. Another irony is the fact that my first encounter with gangs happened twenty-five years ago, and the gang members who confronted me *weren't* Latino, African or Asian. Jack H led his gang, and though they took my money, they backed down from my father. And we despised Jack H because he was a thief and a bully.

SEXISM & READING

 ARK C. BLOOM TIRE STORE was on the corner of 108th and Western, just around the corner from where we lived on 109th St. In those days we had the time to say the entire name—Mark C. Bloom (I can't help but think of Molly Bloom)—as opposed to the way it's now said: Bloom's. In those days the names of stores and associations didn't have the acronymic sex appeal they now have. KFC for Kentucky Fried Chicken. BSA for Boy Scouts of America. JBS for John Birch Society. Mark C. Bloom was important in my personal history because it was on the way to get air in the tires of my new bike, the bike I'd hoped and dreamed for, the bike I'd asked Santa for, that my father and I agreed that I knew there really wasn't a Santa Claus.

The only fast food place around at the time was Tastee Freeze (is it now TF?), where sometimes on summer Friday nights my parents and my older brother and I would walk up Western Avenue, toward Century, all the way to Tastee Freeze, where we'd get Flying Saucers, frozen chocolate covered ice milk in the shape of a saucer from outer space.

On our walks we'd pass Mark C. Bloom, of course, and pass the car wash and the vacant lot. In the back of the car wash was a big wooden bench that was covered by a roof, and where an old black man would shine the shoes of those who had enough money to have their cars washed. Underneath the big wooden bench the old man stored pop bottles. Sometimes he'd give us a few so we could get the deposit and buy candy. I think in those days it was a penny a bottle. And candy bars were a nickel. Also, admission to the Rio Theater's Saturday matinee was 10 cents.

On our side of 108th on the northwest corner, was the bus stop. On summer mornings I used to walk with my mother to the bus stop, where she'd catch the 7:30 bus. She'd wake me around six in the morning, allow me to get my bearings, and then while she prepared for her workday, I'd read to her from a secretarial book. She was trying to improve her shorthand skills so she could get a raise, get a better paying job. Usually she'd take one or two practice tests in the morning before we'd go to the bus stop.

My mother was very attractive, and still is, though time has worked its magic, making her attractive in different ways than those of her youth. She's from New Mexico, and has the light skin the blend of Spanish and Indian blood gives one, and her face is very pretty, with a distinct nose, like a Roman nose but it's not Roman, it's Indian. She took great care of her body, watching her diet and doing moderate exercises, though the standard for what is attractive has dramatically changed since then—think Rita Hayworth vs. Demi Moore.

My mother had the curse of large breasts, I believe. I didn't think of it one way or the other, but I know now that this may be a burden for a woman. I saw the looks my friends gave my sister when she was developing, and know too the way I was affected when I was in the presence of a girl with large breasts.

My father worked the graveyard shift and wouldn't get home until after eight in the morning, after my mother was picked up by the bus, beginning her hour-long ride to work. He was a printer. Most days I'd come home from the bus stop, see my father, eat breakfast, and then have the day to myself. My father was around but my brother and I had strict instructions not to awaken him. Only in an emergency. In my memory it seems my father was always groggy, except on Saturdays, when he'd had a good night's sleep. He worked the graveyard shift many years, enduring the toll it must have taken on his body, not to mention his psyche. He was a good provider, a stoic worker, rarely missing a day.

My mother was the same way, though she worked for a temp agency called Kelly Girls so that she could be around for us when we were growing up. Except that almost every place she'd temp, they'd offer her full-time employment. What happened one day at the bus stop brought it all together: my mother's beauty, my father's work schedule, my accompanying my mother to the bus stop. All these things contributed to my behavior later that afternoon.

I see now that my mother had done the hard studying before we even left the house, and I see that the reason I accompanied her to the bus stop was more for moral support than actual practice in shorthand. As I read from the secretarial text she took shorthand, and wouldn't have to look at the passing motorists. Oftentimes men would yell at her, as I sat next to her on the bus stop bench, and sometimes they'd whistle. I didn't like this but I too learned to ignore them. They weren't particularly menacing. My mother would concentrate on her shorthand and I'd read to her from the book. She would never acknowledge the leers from the passing motorists.

At least this is how I've recreated it from memory, and I don't know whether or not my memory is accurate, whether or not I've recreated it thusly for the sake of my narrative. But there it is: I've connected my behavior on a Friday afternoon with the events of a Friday morning. And this is the reason. Two men in a pickup truck were particularly rude that morning, even yelling obscenities. It's hard to take, even when you're only seven-years old, for I'd been in fist fights with boys for far less. But these were men, and there were two of them, and they passed us, yelling at my mother, she ignoring them, I staring them down.

I thought that was it, the bus would come, my mother would hug me good-bye, and I'd go about my business. This was not to be. The pickup with the two rude men reappeared, on the other side of the street, heading the opposite direction on Western, really riled now, whistling, hooting, saying lewd things to my mother. My mother stopped her shorthand, stared straight ahead, not responding to the low-lifes.

But these men were not finished. They approached us still another time. Except this time they pulled over to the curb, right in front of the bus stop bench, and one man, the one riding shotgun, opened his door as if he was about to get out. He didn't get all the way out, however. He had his feet on the street, but kept his body on the truck's seat. He wore black boots. Scuffed and dented. He kept asking my mother to get in the truck with them. They could have a good time, the man said. You're interested, I know, the man said.

I thought I was brave. I'd already read about the chivalrous behavior of the Knights of the Round Table. I thought
I could protect my mother, should the events dictate. But
then and there I knew I was only a boy against two men
and would be mostly powerless to resist their overwhelming size and weight and animal cunning.

A few motorists honked at the men, as they were block-
ing the right turn path to 108th St. The men weren't in the
least fazed by other motorists' displeasure. They stayed a
few feet from us, thinking they could coax my mother into
the truck.

I'd thought I'd say something, thought I'd try to defend
my mother, and maybe I would have had the men done
anything further. There was nothing physical, it was all
verbal, though their actions were degrading and humiliat-
ing. We'd done nothing to spark the encounter, done nothing to deserve it. Except my mother's looks.

My mother finally said something, something such as,
Leave us alone, and What's the matter with you? benign
things like those. And then the bus came, and the men
drove away.

I hugged my mother good-bye, extremely embarrassed
for what had happened. For my ineffectual behavior. For
my impotence. My father would have never let something
like that occur, right under his nose.

The more I thought about it the angrier I became, until I
was in a real snit by the late afternoon. I couldn't face my
father, after the demeaning encounter, so I just went
straight to Sportsman's Park, on Western and Century, and
played basketball in the cool gym, and shot caroms in the
lobby, and ventured outside in the late afternoon, all the

way to the wading pool, where I mock fought with my friends.

I walked home with a boy who lived near me, in the big apartments behind Mark C. Bloom. And I don't know whether or not I instigated what we did, or if my friend was the bad influence. I really can't say, though I think in retrospect the morning's events fueled my anger and behavior.

I can't get out of what I did either. First we stole a bunch of bottles from underneath the shoeshine man's bench. We took them to the little market up on Western, before Tastee Freeze, getting candy with the deposit.

It was going on six p.m., and the car wash and Mark C. Bloom were closed. Again we went behind the car wash, to the back of the shoeshine stand, and broke the remaining bottles, leaving a mess of shattered glass for the shoeshine man. I think we justified our actions by making disparaging racial remarks about the shoeshine man, who was always pleasant and nice, even going so far as to give us pop bottles so we could get the deposit and buy candy.

And still, my anger hadn't run its course. In the alley behind Mark C. Bloom there were always a bunch of tires. Trade-ins. Before the trash truck hauled them away. No special treatment for tires in those days. Nobody worked past five p.m. at that time, and only half a day on Saturday, and never on Sunday were they open. We rolled some tires from the alley over to the vacant lot and began messing around with them in the dirt. The vacant lot was on a slight hill so you weren't seen from Western Ave. My friend lost one of his tires, and it rolled down onto Western with such speed that we ran away. Nothing happened, however, it didn't hit any cars or anything. But it gave me an idea.

We went back to Mark C. Bloom and took more tires, rolling them to the vacant lot. For some reason I fancied myself lying in wait for that pickup truck, the one that had harassed my mother and me. I imagined the tires were artillery shells, and thought I'd blast that pickup, should I see it. I knew the chances were slim and none that it would reappear but still, I reasoned, it wouldn't hurt to be ready. I had three tires on the hill, ready to launch them onto Western Ave.

My friend got bored after waiting some time for the appearance of the phantom truck. I don't think I even remembered what it looked like. My friend walked behind the lot to the alley and called for me. Traffic was stopped on Western. I launched my tires. And ran.

As I got to the alley, I saw that traffic was again moving on the busy street. My tires were gaining momentum as they flowed off the dirt hill, over the sidewalk, jumping the curb. Immediately they were in the midst of moving cars. One hit the driver's side door of a car, making a big dent in it. Someone else squealed their brakes, almost getting rear-ended, but missing the runaway tire. The third artillery round made it all the way across the street, collapsing harmlessly against a building.

A few motorists were out of their cars, looking in my direction. I ran, passing my friend, cutting up the next alley, running as far as the church, where my friend caught up with me. We stealthily made our way to his apartment, which was just off the alley. After an appropriate amount of time, I crossed 108th Street, making my way home, where I immediately went into the backyard.

My mother was home cooking dinner, I could smell the

fish frying—Catholics still ate fish on Friday in those days—and the potatoes, and I could hear her speaking with my father. I went out to the back lawn, without greeting my parents, and lay under the avocado tree with my dog. After a time I got bored so I began spinning on the grass, making myself dizzy. I collapsed onto the lawn and watched the clouds above me spin, and heard the traffic sounds down on Western begin to diminish.

I don't know exactly what my mother said to my father that night, probably she just told him the truth, but shortly later he bought an old junker car, which he drove to work, and my mother took the good family car when she was employed. I never could face the shoeshine man again, never went back to take more bottles, or to receive them as gifts. I never took tires from the back of Mark C. Bloom again either. I also don't recall waiting at the bus stop with my mother ever again.

TAGGING AND THE FACTS OF LIFE

W<small>E DIDN'T CALL IT TAGGING.</small> Writing on the walls was what it was called, and I'd never done it, never desired to do so, for there was no romance associated with the act. So when I was caught in the act by the Washington High School security guard, with Larry J and Lenny M, my family was pretty taken aback. I did well in school. So well that there was a lot of pressure on my parents to allow me to skip a grade. I was also very good in sports.

I'll always remember that day. A lovely Sunday afternoon, the air a little crisp with autumn, the sky a wonderful slate blue, with a few lazy clouds high up. And Larry J leaning over his handiwork, trying in vain to hide the blue spray paint letters that even then dripped down, down, onto the pristine enamel drinking fountain. The reason he leaned over to cover what he'd just written was that suddenly before us was the tallest man I'd ever seen, dressed in a long black coat, wearing a black fedora, restraining a nasty-looking German shepherd dog. The man and the dog had snuck up on us.

Larry had just written "fuck you" on the long porcelain drinking fountain and the blue paint slid down its surface like ice cream melting down a drain.

You boys have been pretty busy, the detective said. He later told us he was a detective, hired by the principal to stop vandalism on the campus.

Not really, Larry said.

The detective said, I've been following you for about an hour.

Catch the guys who gave us the paint, Larry said. At the time, I thought that was quick thinking. His eight-year-old body wasn't large enough to cover the words he'd spray painted. So his hands were out in front of him in an attempt to camouflage his graffito.

Lenny M was eleven, I was going to be nine in a few months, after Christmas, and after the New Year. Lenny didn't say anything. He was very big for his age, larger than most adults, though he wasn't bigger than this dreary man who stood at attention with his attack dog. Running was not an option.

The detective ignored Larry's attempt to deflect blame, instead taking our names and writing them in a little notebook. He confiscated our spray paint after which he took us on a tour of our vandalism. The worst part was the new science building, which was not yet operational, though it would be shortly, brand spanking new. I felt bad when things were put in this perspective.

It was dusk by the time the detective took us into the administration office, where he called the principal, the police, and our parents. Our parents would have been worried since we were supposed to have been home some time ago. Being late was the least of our troubles.

♦

It happened like this: three boys playing together on a Sunday. Larry's mother dropped him off at my house. Lenny lived across the street and catty-corner to me on 109th Street, just off Western Avenue. We walked down to Imperial Highway, looking at the Rio Theater's marquee. We skirted the Devil's Dips, the huge field that would later become Southwest College, looking for snakes. Once I'd seen a king snake fight a rattlesnake. Things happened at Devil's Dips. A friend's older brother was hit on the head with a wrench while in a fight there. He had brain damage. And someone else had gone over his handlebars while racing down a particularly steep hill, and had broken his sternum, a bloody mess. Hobos even lived by the train overpass, the source of the lonely wail of the whistle late at night. I wasn't allowed to go to the Devil's Dips.

But I was doing many things that day that I wasn't supposed to be doing. Ergo the next series of events played themselves out capriciously. For when we returned home, we came across two girls who were visiting a neighbor. They were having cookies and milk and offered us some. We accepted, going in the backyard with them. That set in motion the sequence of events that put us in the principal's office with a policeman, a principal, a detective, and our parents. The worst trouble I'd ever gotten in.

But it *really* began, I guess, before that day, before we entered the backyard with the girls who were visiting a neighbor. I knew that babies came from inside a woman. Yet I thought that babies came out through the woman's stomach. Lenny M set me straight. I knew that men and women were built differently, and that a woman didn't have a penis. Still, I thought the vagina was primarily for urination—I tried to put it in terms I could understand. I didn't know that it was the entry to the birth canal.

Lenny went on to tell me how men and women had sex to create a child, and as if by magic, my dog was in heat. We let her mate with Lenny's dog, and watched a sort of live visual aid, Lenny providing the commentary in his all-knowing and whispering eleven-year-old voice.

The whole deal sickened and excited me.

But I was different after the mating display, after Lenny explained the facts of life to me. I couldn't imagine my parents doing something so intrinsically barbaric and animalistic to each other, and I half doubted Lenny. I'd seen my dog and his dog, however, and three months later my dog had a litter of pups, conclusive proof as to Lenny's pontificating.

After we ate the cookies and milk, the girls began playing on the backyard swingset. They were swinging and climbing on the frame of the swing. One of the girls hung upside down from the crossbar. We all saw her underpants. Then her friend did a similar maneuver by standing up in the swingset while going back and forth lifting her dress to show her panties. We were getting pretty worked up by then, and the girls knew it, I think, but they continued their dance of seduction.

And then out of nowhere adults appeared. Must have seen what was going on as we were immediately escorted to the front sidewalk, and the girls taken inside.

The garage door was open, a big old car still ticking with heat from its drive, and Lenny saw some cans of spray paint on a shelf. We went into the garage and took a few cans of paint.

We were worked up.

And with free time. So we ended up at Washington High School, up the street from where I lived. On a glorious Sunday afternoon. And all sexed out by those girls.

The first thing Lenny wrote was "fuck." Seemed the reasonable word, given the prior events. Larry and I followed suit. Then we began wandering the halls, writing our profanities with abandon and glee, and thought about the white underpants the girls wore.

◆

We were released to our parents. They had cut a deal with the principal. We had to scrub the graffiti during school hours, and pay restitution. That placated the principal. I was grounded for a month. And I knew I'd get a whipping.

My father administered the whipping as soon as we arrived home. The only thing he said to me was, I suppose you know what that word means. He said it with a sadness and disappointment, a poignancy that made me feel badly. He wanted to explain the intricacies of life, I was sure, and I hadn't allowed him the chance. I'd embarrassed him by writing what I wrote in public.

I got a good whipping, my ass burned, and I cried alone on my bed. The rest of the punishment would be easy, I figured. There was a further aspect which didn't upset me too much at the time. I could no longer play with Lenny. Still, I thought I'd gotten off easily.

◆

40

Lenny's mother didn't work so she took us to do the cleaning one afternoon the following week. We had scrub brushes, detergent, vinyl gloves, and paint remover. We didn't wear our best clothes.

And we thought it was really cool that they were "punishing" us by making us leave school early, to do our penance. Our teachers had lectured in our classes about what a terrible thing it is to destroy property that doesn't belong to you, and it was with a certain notoriety that we were escorted off our school grounds, Woodcrest Elementary School, and taken to Washington High School. None of our peers thought what we'd done was funny. We had defaced the new high school building, the science building no less! Almost treason in those days, for science was to be our deliverance from the "red threat." Nobody admired us for our actions.

It got worse at the high school. Students actually jeered us as we cleaned. And this: That damn paint wouldn't come off no matter how hard we scrubbed. We scrubbed into the early evening, glad when school was long over and most of the students were gone.

♦

I didn't see Larry anymore, only at Sportsman's Park. His mother wouldn't bring him to my house any longer, and I didn't ask to go to his house. Lenny started smoking. He had a girlfriend who had her hair piled high on her head. Those girls who visited down the street never were in the neighborhood again.

Did all of it have to do with the raging pre-pubescent

hormones of three unsupervised boys? Was it the fault of the girls who knew they were working us up? Sure, blame Eve, you'll say. And there's something to your comment. Yet Eve didn't get the whipping. (She has, to be sure, taken a thrashing, for a long, long time.)

I'd never been the recipient of a public humiliation before, or since, but after having undergone one, knew I'd never write on the walls again.

My father, before he administered my physical punishment, said nobody was to blame for my actions except me. If I wished to do those kinds of things, I'd also have to be willing to take the punishment.

My father only whipped my older brother and me when we'd done something particularly outrageous. My writing graffiti certainly fell into this category. We were not supposed to call attention to ourselves, and negative attention was definitely a bad thing.

I have a four-year old son, and I've never once administered corporal punishment to him. And I don't know what I'll do when I'm faced with disciplining or punishing him for his errant behavior. I don't believe in physical violence, and corporal punishment is just that, even if given to a loved one by a loved one. But I hope I can somehow come up with the appropriate punishment, the punishment that fits the crime, so that he will learn the lesson the first time out, as I did.

MVP

As I RODE THE BUS from South Los Angeles toward East Los Angeles to visit my grandparents, I thought I was pretty cool. There was to be a banquet at Sportsman's Park next weekend; I would receive the most valuable player trophy for football, the highest honor for a young player. And my parents trusted me enough to take the bus across town, on my own, to spend the night with my grandmother. My grandmother would take me to the movies, a matinee, and she would take me shopping, buying me virtually anything I wanted.

The reason I got to go on my own to my grandmother's, I suppose, was because my brother, who was the first-born child of the entire family, always got the most lavish gifts for Christmas. My mother and aunt had organized a boycott last Easter, for the disparity in the gifts between what my brother got compared with my loot was really something. For intstance, I might get a soap on a rope from my grandmother while my brother might get slacks, a sweater vest, and a dress shirt! So the compromise was that I'd get to visit my grandmother from time to time and have my own private shopping spree, which I wouldn't get if things were left as they were.

I rode the bus that Saturday morning content and excited about my forthcoming prospects: toys and clothes; next weekend I'd be honored at the Sportsman's Park Banquet. Last year's football banquet had Jack Kemp as a presenter—he'd handed out the trophies, though he wasn't a bigshot government person back then, he was a good quarterback in the fledging AFL. I fantasized that maybe Johnny Unitas might visit our little park, or maybe Crazy Legs Hirsch from our very own Rams, though he was retired.

There weren't many passengers on the bus that morning, though people did ride the buses more often than now, or so it seemed to me because the bus was a part of our lives in a way that it no longer is. Maybe I'm naïve, thinking that just because I did something meant that others did as well. I came out of my reverie when the bus driver announced the street where I'd be transferring.

My mother wrote careful instructions, folded and put them in my front pocket, should I need a reminder of my route. My parents told me to tell each bus driver where I'd need to transfer. They told me the bus drivers would look out for me, and they did. Sit behind the bus driver, my father said.

The city looked much the same to me as we moved closer and closer to its center, except there were more commercial buildings and fewer houses. There were even a few factories, and the streets now seemed dirtier—it was different.

I got off the bus with my transfer token in hand, walked to the opposite corner, where I'd catch the next bus. My mother had it all worked out so I wouldn't wait long at any one place. I was to call my parents as soon as I arrived at my grandmother's apartment. Or call from a pay phone should I have the need.

The year before my football team hadn't done that well. Our "coach" had absconded with the uniform money, leaving the team coachless and in shock. Jerry G, the Park Director, and graduate student at Pepperdine University, coached us, and we had a respectable record, all things considered, even though we played without team jerseys—our parents had already put out ten dollars for them and weren't about to do so again. It was really something for me to go from a coachless, jerseyless season to being named the league's most valuable player. I was proud of the honor. I did well in school too. The teachers and school principal at Woodcrest Elementary once again approached my parents about my skipping a grade, but my parents said no, they wanted me to be with children my own age. My parents both worked, neither having a college degree.

Before I bore you with my successes, let me introduce the narrative's antagonist: The Fever. What my friends, Sheldon C and Tom G, called our stealing. It had started some months back when we'd wanted barbecue potato chips and had no money. Tom or Sheldon, I forget which one, went into a market wearing a baggy sweatshirt, and stole a large bag of potato chips. Somebody's friend's brother had taught them to steal. Look at magazines or something, act casual, and wear baggy clothes, though not too baggy for that would call attention to you.

The reason we called it The Fever was because even at our young age we knew the process had the better of us, sort of like gambling or something. And we were gambling—that we wouldn't get caught. Where the thrill lay. The heart of The Fever.

The first few times we rationalized our thievery as "necessity." We'd be at the park, say, and would be hungry, and wouldn't want to ride our bikes all the way home to eat lunch. So we'd go into a store, steal a candy bar, or a bag of potato chips, or some Twinkies, whatever caught our fancy. It was easy to steal when there were two or three boys and only one proprietor. Tom and Sheldon were a year older than I, and they instructed me well—soon the three of us were going our merry thieving ways, grabbing everything we desired, mostly junky food, however. Still, it was a means to create excitement, a way to pass the long days of summer, when you stayed away from home all day to show how big you were.

Toward the end of summer I got caught. There was a market right across Western, opposite Sportsman's Park, which was on the corner of Western and Century in South Los Angeles, not too far from Watts, just up Century Boulevard. Sportsman's Park is now called Jesse Owens Park. The kids from the park always bought soft drinks and candy from the market. So this one day I went in with some teammates on the all-stars with me. Some sporting goods store had donated sports bags, small valises for us to carry our gloves and cleats and things in, and I thought I'd put some food in the bag. No big deal. I'd done it before with small things.

While in the store and walking the aisles, I got the bright idea to stick an entire cake in the bag. Those all-star bags were status symbols so we'd often carry them even if they held no equipment. The bag was empty, the cake was in. That simple. My teammates circled like sharks, putting whatever they wanted to eat in their bags.

We met up at the checkout counter, where we bought some penny gum, or something similarly absurd, and made for the door. Just outside the doorway the manager lay in wait. He stopped us. Said we'd stolen numerous items, and that he was taking us back into the store, which he did.

He interviewed us separately, never allowing us to talk among ourselves to get our stories to match, if we had any stories, which we didn't. I don't know what those other boys said to the manager. I told him the truth, that my parents both worked, there was no reason for me to steal, and I was sorry. I was. And scared. I thought he'd call the police. Then my parents would become involved.

After he talked with me, the manager said I was a good boy, and that I shouldn't be hanging around with those other boys. They were troublemakers, he said. They're not nice boys, he said. He further said that he was letting us go, because I was a decent boy. But I had to promise not to steal anymore, and never to come in his store again.

I remembered that time as I rode the bus, transferring once again, taking the bus to Wabash, which turned into City Terrace Drive, where my grandmother lived, City Terrace. When I'd be breaking one of my promises to that manager.

My grandmother waited for me at the bus stop on City Terrace Drive, and she helped me with the bag of things my mother had sent. What was in the bag I hadn't bothered to look at. I carried my all-star bag up the steep hill to her apartment, where my grandmother made me eat another breakfast, though this time it was chorizo and fried eggs and a pork chop. And homemade corn tortillas, the kind I loved. I was stuffed, but that was the way it was when you visited your grandmother—you ate. She cooked, you ate. In those days she was still young, though she seemed ancient to me. She was short and wore cotton dresses and her hair was dark brown, and she had the high cheekbones my father and grandfather have, very Indian-looking.

After she cooked my food she changed into better clothes, and once again we walked down the hill to the bus stop. We would ride the bus across the Los Angeles River to downtown Los Angeles. We didn't wait long, for there were buses everywhere, or so it seemed to me.

At the back of the bus were two cholos, boys a little older than I, wearing baggy clothes, and one of them had a hair net over his head and forehead, and they looked at me with pure hatred. They were saying things in Spanish in street slang that I couldn't quite translate. I did know, however, that they were making fun of me. My grandmother finally had enough of their laughing and dirty talk. She told them to shut their mouths. In Spanish. This really got them going, and my grandmother as well, but nothing much came of it.

I was big for my age, well-coordinated, smart in school, and an MVP. I had it all over those low-life cholos who would never amount to anything. They were probably just jealous of my clothes or something, since I wasn't from the area and dressed differently. I wore slacks and a sweater and dress shoes. They wore chino pants frayed at the bottoms, huge Sir Guy wool shirts, and French toed shoes. I was somebody. I was getting a trophy next Saturday, at the culmination of the football banquet. I wasn't scared of those punks, I told myself. In reality I was scared big time of those boys; they could have eaten me for breakfast, had they desired. I was glad I was with my grandmother, the reason they began making fun of me in the first place. The cholos got off the bus at Dog Town, the public housing tenements.

The Los Angeles River was a trickle of water, and for this everyone makes fun of it. But this is a semi-arid environment. Rivers only flow after a rain, or when the snow melts in the mountains. It makes as much sense to make fun of a dry wash in a desert as it would to call a tree filthy when it's losing its leaves in autumn. Both functions are perfect for the respective environments.

We crossed the bridge, getting off the bus at Broadway. Then my Saturday began in earnest. Right off the bat I got an Orange Julius. We walked the crowded downtown streets, my grandmother doing some of her shopping while getting me a baseball cap, Dodgers, and almost getting me a football uniform, Rams, though I was too big to wear it, and demurred.

We went to a matinee where we saw *The Creature From the Black Lagoon*. My grandmother called it ugly, in Spanish. She didn't like the movie at all. I ate popcorn and bon-bons during the movie, but was still hungry. We then ate at a cafeteria.

After eating, we went to The Broadway for the grand finale. I could have virtually anything I desired. Yet for some reason I thought of The Fever, and of my friends, Sheldon and Tom, how I would dazzle them with my exploits of thievery, and forgot all about getting caught at the market and of my promises to the manager. I began putting small things in the shopping bag I carried, stupid things like socks and handkerchiefs, things my grandmother would gladly pay for, or things that might turn up under the Christmas tree, precipitating the boycott. And here I was stealing them! I had to get into a better section of the store. I told my grandmother I would meet her in the camera department; she agreed since she needed some women's things anyway, and was probably embarrassed to buy them with me in tow.

It had been a tricky business, stealing while with my grandmother—not only did I have to be on the guard for store personnel, but I also had to watch for her. The camera department was on a different floor so I took the escalator. Free. And excited. As I approached a display of small boxes that had spy cameras in them, I decided that I would strike quickly, before the clerks had a chance to be aware of me. I walked right up to the display, dropped one small box into the shopping bag I'd put at my feet, and placed another box back on the display. It was quick, it was smooth. I was good.

Unfortunately my grandmother had followed to give me some cash in case I wished to purchase something while out of her presence. She came up behind me, wrenched my arm, and then emptied my shopping bag. She put the small camera back on the display, went through the other items I had stolen, and marched me around the store, replacing the items in their proper places.

On the bus ride back to her apartment she asked me why I would do such a thing. I just shrugged, wishing the cholos were around to deflect attention away from me.

It was early evening by the time we got back to her apartment. My grandfather was home from work, but he didn't get too worked up over the fact that I was a thief. My father and mother did, however, for even though I was to spend the night, they arrived around nine p.m. and whisked me home.

My older brother must have liked the fact that for once I was in trouble. Usually he was the one who messed up. Last spring he had cheated on his report card and transposed his grades, D's into A's, and my proud parents only found out when they attended open house at the school. I liked his huevos, his chutzpah. He was sick of my good grades and excellence in sports. Still, he didn't seem too happy to see me in this much trouble. He left the room we shared, left me alone to face my punishment the way he'd taken his for changing his grades.

My father and mother spoke for some time before my father entered my room. He began by asking me why I would steal when my grandmother was buying me so many things. I didn't have an answer. I couldn't tell him about The Fever. I'd be in even more trouble. I remained mute. My father told me that he and my mother worked hard to give me the things they did, and he was aware that I didn't get everything I wanted or needed, still, he said, I didn't go without. My father told me that nobody in his family would be a thief. He told me I was grounded for a month, that the only time I could go outside was to do my chores or to go to school, other than that I was to stay in my room. I asked him about the banquet next weekend. He said I didn't deserve to go. I couldn't go anywhere for an entire month. And then I got a hard whipping with his belt.

I cried after my whipping, though not so much from my burning butt and legs. No, I cried because I wouldn't be able to receive my trophy. I wouldn't be able to stand up in front of everyone and have them applaud me for my achievements. That was mainly why I cried. I lay on my single bed in my room with the stark white light on overhead, thinking what might have been. It was quite late when my brother came in to bed, and turned off the light.

After my sentence was served, I rode my bike to the park on a Saturday morning. Jerry G, the Park Director, was in his office. I said hello to him. He asked me if I were okay, and said they'd missed me at the banquet. I told him that I couldn't make it but that I had come for my trophy. It was on the shelf above his desk. He smiled when he handed it to me, though there was no handshake, and I knew, just knew, that he'd talked with my father. No applause either.

I held that trophy and examined every inch of its golden surface. It was something. Wood base, golden football player. The little plaque on the front said: MVP, Boys Football, Sportsman's Park. After an awkward time of silence, Jerry G said, Basketball sign-ups are next week.

I rode my bike home along Western, passing the market where the manager had let us off because I was a good kid. I didn't feel very "good." In fact, I didn't show my trophy to any of my family until my father came in my room and asked if he could see it.

OF CHOLOS AND SURFERS

THE ONLY STORE AROUND that had this new magazine was a Food Giant on Vermont Avenue, just off Imperial. *Surfer Quarterly*, it was then called. Now it's *Surfer* and they've celebrated their thirtieth anniversary. Sheldon made the discovery by chance when he'd gone shopping with his mother, who needed something found only at Food Giant. Normally we didn't go that far east to shop; we went west toward Crenshaw, to the nicer part of town.

We all wanted to be surfers, in fact called ourselves surfers even though we never made it to the beach, though it was less than ten miles away. One of the ways you could become a surfer was to own an issue of *Surfer Quarterly*. Since there had been only a few prior issues, I was hot to get the new one. To be a surfer you also had to wear baggy shorts, large Penney's Towncraft T-shirts, and go barefoot, no matter how much the hot sidewalks burned your soles.

That summer in the early sixties I was doing odd jobs around the house for my parents: weeding; painting the eaves; baby-sitting during the daytime. I was earning money so that I could buy Lenny M's surfboard, another way to be a surfer. It was a Velzy-Jacobs, ten feet six inches long, twenty-four inches wide, and it had the coolest red oval decal.

Now Lenny and I no longer saw much of each other, though he still looked out for me. A strange thing happened to Lenny the previous school year. He grew. Like the green giant or something. He was over six feet tall and the older guys would let him hang out with them. So Lenny had become sort of a hood, wearing huge Sir Guy wool shirts, baggy khaki pants with the cuffs rolled, and French-toed black shoes. He drank wine, even getting drunk in the daytime with his hoodlum friends. Lenny was now respected, feared, even, by some of the parents and no longer needed or desired to own a surfboard—he was going in the opposite direction. There were two distinct paths in my neighborhood: hood or surfer.

I was entering junior high school in a month, and I still hung out with Sheldon C and Tom G. They lived by Morningside Heights, and their houses were more expensive than mine, and they'd both been surfers before I'd aspired toward such a life. Sheldon and Tom wore their hair long, constantly cranking their heads back to keep their bangs out of their eyes. My parents wouldn't let hair grow over my ears no matter how much I argued with them. But I was the one buying a surfboard. Lenny was holding it for me. My parents would match any money I saved over the summer.

Yet *Surfer Quarterly* was more tangible since it only cost one dollar. Lenny's Velzy-Jacobs was forty-five dollars, quite a large sum for the time. The issue then became one of how to obtain the object of desire. The Food Giant on Vermont was reachable by bike, but I was no longer allowed to ride up there. Not since my older brother had gone to the Southside Theatre one Saturday and had seen a boy get knifed because of his skin color. Vermont was a tough area, though some of the kids I went to school with lived up there and they weren't any different from us. Yet none of them wished to be surfers, I don't think.

What was needed was for me to include my father in the negotiation. I wasn't allowed to ride my bike to Vermont, I reasoned with him. Therefore, he should drive me. He agreed with me and that was that. Except I had to wait until the following Friday when he didn't have to work his usual graveyard shift.

In the late afternoons I'd go to Sportsman's Park, where I'd virtually grown up. I made the all-stars in baseball, basketball, and football. Our first opponent on the path to the city championships was always Will Rogers Park in Watts (now called Ted Watkins Park). Sheldon and Tom and I had been on the same teams. Sometimes I'd see them in the afternoons before we'd have to return home for dinner. We'd pore over Sheldon's issue of *Surfer* while sitting in the bleachers next to the baseball diamond. If it was too hot we'd go in the wading pool, though we were getting too old for that scene since mostly women and kids used it.

When Friday afternoon arrived and my father had showered and my mother had returned from work, I reminded my father of our agreement. We drove the neighborhood streets up to Vermont, passing Washington High School, Normandie Avenue, Woodcrest Elementary School and so on. We spoke mostly of me. Was I looking forward to attending Henry Clay Junior High? Would I still be in accelerated classes? My teachers and the principal talked each year with my parents about the possiblity of my skipping a grade but my parents always said no.

Just as my father had exhausted his repertoire of school questions, we arrived at the Food Giant. After parking in the back lot, we entered the store and made for the liquor section, where the magazines were housed. I stood in front of the rack, butterflies of expectations overtaking my stomach while my father bought himself some beer. I knew immediately when I found the magazine. It looked like a square of water was floating in the air. An ocean-blue cover with a huge wave completely engulfing a surfer with the headline—BANZAI PIPELINE. I held the magazine with great reverence, as if I were holding something of spiritual value, which it was.

Is that it? my father asked. He held a quart of Hamm's in each hand, his Friday night's allotment.

Yes, I said.

At the counter my father took the magazine from me, leafing through it too casually, I thought. I could see the bulging veins in his powerful forearms, and saw too the solid bumps that were his biceps.

Looks like a crazy thing to do, he said, finally placing the magazine on the counter next to the beer. My father, the practical provider, the person whose closet was pristine for lack of clothes, though the ones he did own were stylish, but not expensive. This was why he drank beer from quart bottles—it was cheaper that way. I know now how difficult it must have been raising four children on the hourly wages my parents made.

The man at the counter rang up the purchases, stopping for a moment to look at the *Surfer*. He smiled.

Eres Mexicano? my father asked him.

Sí, como no? the man answered.

Then my father and the store clerk began poking fun at my magazine in Spanish, nothing too mean, but ranking it as silly adolescent nonsense.

When we got back in the car I asked my father why he always asked certain people if they were Mexican. He only asked men who obviously were, thus knowing in advance their answers. He shrugged his shoulders and said he didn't know. It was a way of initiating conversation, he said. Well, it was embarrassing for me, I told him. Because I held the magazine in my lap, I was able to let my father off the hook. It was more important that I give it a quick thumb-through as we drove home. The *Surfer* was far more interesting for me as a twelve-year-old than the larger issues of race.

I spent the entire Friday evening holed up in my room, poring over the magazine, not even interested in eating popcorn or watching *77 Sunset Strip*, our familial Friday night ritual. By the next morning I had almost memorized every photo caption and their sequence. I spoke with Sheldon on the phone and he and Tom were meeting me later at Sportsman's Park. I did my chores in a self-absorbed trance, waiting for the time when I could share my treasure with my friends. My mother made me eat lunch before I was finally able to leave.

Walking the long walk along Western Avenue toward Century and glancing at the photos in the magazine, I didn't pay attention to the cholo whom I passed on the sidewalk. I should have been more aware, but was too preoccupied. So there I was, in a street confrontation before I knew what had happened.

You a surfer? he said with disdain. He said it the way you start to say chocolate, but "churfer" isn't quite it either.

I stopped and turned to face him. He wore a wool watch cap pulled down onto his eyebrows, a long Sir Guy wool shirt with the top button buttoned and all the rest unbuttoned, khaki pants so long they were frayed at the bottoms and so baggy I couldn't see his shoes. I wore Bermuda shorts and a large Towncraft T-shirt. I was barefoot. My parents wouldn't let hair grow over my ears. Cholo meets surfer. Not a good thing. As he clenched his fists I saw a black cross tattooed onto the fleshy part of his hand.

His question was not like my father's. My father, I now sensed, wanted a common bond upon which to get closer to strangers. This guy was Mexican American, and he wanted to fight me because I wore the outfit of a surfer.

I rolled the magazine in a futile attempt to hide it, but the cholo viewed this action as an escalation with a perceived weapon. It wasn't that I was overly afraid of him, though fear can work to your advantage if used correctly. I was big for my age, and had been in many fights. The problem was this: I was hurrying off to see my friends, to share something important with them, walking on a summer day, and I didn't feel like rolling on the ground with some stranger because he'd decided we must do so. Why did he get to dictate when or where I would fight? There was another consideration, one more utilitarian. Who knew what sort of weapons he had under all that baggy clothing. A rat-tail comb at the least. More likely a knife because in those days guns weren't that common.

At Woodcrest Elementary School there was a recently arrived Dutch Indonesian immigrant population. One of the most vicious fights I had ever seen was the one when Victor V fought his own cousin. And the toughest fight I'd ever been in was against Julio A over something during a basketball game. There must be some element of self-loathing which propels us to fight those of our own ethnicity with a particular ferocity.

Just before the cholo was going to initiate the fight, I said, I'm Mexican. New Mexican, actually, but I didn't say this. I didn't say, American of Mexican descent, though this is the case.

He seemed unable to process this new information. How could someone be Mexican and dress like a surfer? He looked at me again, this time seeing beyond the clothes I wore. He nodded slightly.

This revelation, this recognition verbalized, molded me in the years to come. A surfer with a peeled nose and a Karmann Ghia with surf racks driving down Whittier Boulevard in East L.A. to visit my grandparents. The imagery of a surfer in the midst of cholos would recur throughtout my life.

When I began attending junior high school, there was a boy nicknamed Niño, who limped around the school yard one day. I discovered the reason for his limp when I went to the bathroom and he had a rifle pointed at boys and was taking their money. I fell in love with a girl named Shirley P, the younger sister of a local surfboard maker. I saw her in her brother's shop after school but she had no idea I loved her. That fall the gang escalation in my neighborhood became so pronounced my parents decided to move. We sold our house very quickly and moved to Huntington Beach and none of us could sleep at night for the quiet. We were surrounded by corn fields and strawberry fields and tomato fields. As a bribe for our sudden move my parents chipped in much more than matching funds so I could buy Lenny M's surfboard. I almost drowned in the big waves of a late autumn south swell, the first time I went out on the Velzy-Jacobs. But later, after I'd surfed for a few years, I expertly rode the waves next to the pier, surfing with new friends.

But I've jumped ahead of myself. I must return to the cholo who is about to attack. But there isn't any more to tell about the incident. We didn't fight that summer's day over thirty years ago. In fact, I never fought another of my own race, and don't know if this was a conscious decision or if circumstances dictated it. As luck would have it, I only fought a few more times during my adolescence, and did so only when attacked.

My father's question, which he'd asked numerous people so long ago taught me these things. The reason he had to ask was because he and my mother had left the safe confines of their Boyle Heights upbringing. They had thrust themselves and their children into what was called at the time the melting pot of Los Angeles. They bought the post World War II American dream of assimilation. I was a pioneer in the sociological sense in that I had no distinct ethnic piece of geography for which my pride and honor depended. Cast adrift in the city streets. Something gained, something lost. I couldn't return to my ethnic neighborhood, but I could be a surfer. And I didn't have to fight for ethnic pride over my city street. The neighborhood kids did, however, stick together, though this was not based upon race. It was a necessity. The older guys would step forward to protect the younger ones. That was how it was done.

The most important thing I learned was that I could do just about anything I wished, within reason. I could be a surfer, if I chose, and even cholos would respect my decision. During my adolescence I went to my grandparents' house for all the holidays. They lived in East Los Angeles. When I was old enough to drive I went on my own, sometimes with a girlfriend. I was able to observe my Los Angeles Mexican heritage, taking a date to the Placita for Easter service and then having lunch at Olvera Street. An Orange County girl who had no idea this part of Los Angeles existed.

PEE WEE & MAKAO & THE JUNGLE

I'LL ALWAYS REMEMBER high school graduation. My parents gave me a round-trip ticket to Hawaii. My friend Greg W also got a ticket from his father—we would fly over together later in the summer. The agreement was that we'd return in time to enroll in community college—there was a small war going on at the time, and if you weren't in college you'd be drafted. I was just out of high school, I didn't want to fight in a war.

The night of graduation was bittersweet at best. I had recently broken up with my girlfriend (she broke up with me, for I'm like a dog, loyal and stupid, and I'd probably still be with her had she not broken it off). The graduating class at Marina High School in Huntington Beach would attend Disneyland for the all-night party. Most everyone was going with a date, and I couldn't bear to go after having just broken up with my girlfriend. We'd gone to the senior prom together, and had a photograph of us taken under the flower-covered arch, and we struck some sort of cute adolescent pose together, she against my shoulder, I with my arms around her. In those days you didn't have to rent a limousine to impress your date. I had a '56 Volkswagen. My father had a new yellow Karmann Ghia, which he loaned me for the evening. Ten years later, at the high school reunion, I drove the same Karmann Ghia, except now the car belonged to me, and I was with my friend Brad, and I saw my high school girlfriend, even sat with her and her friends for dinner, and the women were all married and mothers, and they wore loose-fitting dresses, for they were no longer high school girls, but women tending small children, and my high school girlfriend rubbed my leg underneath the table, in spite of the fact that she was married, and I still liked her.

After the graduation ceremony at the high school, John P's parents were having a party for a few of their son's friends and parents. My parents attended. We had a champagne toast, the first time I drank with my parents. Some time during the party I found myself alone with my father. He told me to enjoy my time now. It's going to go very fast, your life will, my father told me that night. And he was right.

John P and I stayed an appropriate amount of time with the parents then we changed out of our suits and went to another party. In John's GTO. Sixty-five, gray and fast. Though my heart wasn't in it, we went to a few parties, and then drove around talking and smoking, ending up at Denny's at three in the morning, where we ate breakfast. You were supposed to stay out all night the night of your high school graduation, but John and I had nowhere else to go so we went home.

The following week I began looking for a job. I needed to make money for the Hawaii trip. My mother got me a job with her former temp agency, and I got a few weeks of cleaning machinery for minimum wage. After that job I looked in Newport Beach at the docks. Someone told me to try the factory where they built Newport Sailboats, which was inland, between Fountain Valley and Santa Ana. I drove there and got on. Faring keels, sanding fiberglass, doing all the things needed to be done to get the boats in the water.

A guy named Mac was foreman. The second in command was a guy named Pete, and there was another man who did wiring and finish. I was the general go'fer. The other side of the big tilt-up building was where they did the molds. Everyone working with the "hot" fiberglass was Mexican, from the other side.

We also got small fiberglass orders, custom things of between thirty and fifty. One such order was for projector covers. After things come out of a mold they have a seam where the molds fit together. Mac told me to sand the seams on all the projector covers. I must have been asleep at the wheel, for I sanded those covers way too much, making them look worse than with their original seam. Most of them were now unusable, and Mac chewed me out good, which I expected and could take. When he was finished yelling at me he mimicked me giving him my lame excuse. That I wouldn't take. So I gave him notice on the spot. Pete tried to talk me into staying, but when I told him I was going to Hawaii, he understood. I had a small bank account after working about six weeks making sailboats, and I also had some things to get in order before the trip.

◆

Greg W's father and my parents and another guy who invited himself along with us and who had a brother living on the North Shore of Oahu all went to the Los Angeles Airport one early morning in mid-July. It was hard for me to leave my parents; it was the first time I'd done so, but we said our good-byes, boarded the plane, and took off over the smog-obscured ocean.

Getting off the jet after having left a semi-arid environment to arrive in a tropical one is like jumping into an overheated pool. It's this sudden overwhelming sensation, like nothing you've ever felt. And the light is so bright, and the clouds so big, and the sky and the ocean so merged, it's a feeling one only encounters once to remember it forever.

Our friend called his brother, who sent a girl to pick us up at the airport. We drove past pineapple fields and past red dirt, all the way out to the country, to Sunset Beach. The house where we'd stay was alive with activity—there was to be a luau that night. People arrived from all the neighboring islands, and many had come all the way from the mainland, as we had, though we didn't come expressly for the luau. There were girls and women and guys and men everywhere, doing all sorts of organizational tasks. Greg and I and a few girls went swimming in the lake-still bay where in the winter the waves are towering, crashing waterfalls.

There were a lot of drugs at the luau, not many local people, and late at night a group of people from Kauai took over the house and began chanting. Om, they said in unison, over and over. For hours.

Greg and our friend and I took our sleeping bags down to the sand and went to sleep.

I awoke early the next morning, just after dawn, when there were still night shadows, and the trees and foliage echoed some enchanted land, and I could hear water lapping the shore. The mosquitoes had kept me from getting much sleep and I was hot in the sleeping bag so I made my way to the water.

Nobody from the house was stirring, though there must have been well over a hundred people sleeping in it and on the surrounding grounds. It felt as if I were the only person in heaven. I noticed a movement down the beach, in the water, and it took me some time to figure out what I was seeing. I didn't know if the scene was "real" or not.

I gravitated toward the movement, as if there were some sort of knowledge that would be imparted to me, and I was correct. An old man was teaching a child of seven or so how to cast a net in shallow water. They were fishing. They were sharing a skill, the most sacred of skills, the act of providing food. The grandfather was patient—I cooked up a scenario whereby this was a grandfather and grandson— because again and again the child would botch the cast. Over and over the grandfather would gently show the boy how to cast the net. They didn't seem to mind that I was watching, though they didn't acknowledge my existence, and I'm sure I didn't exist for them. For some reason watching these two people, one old, one young, made me hopeful and melancholy. I thought of my father someday teaching my own son such things.

And I also had an unusual, unsettled feeling about the task the grandfather and grandson were performing juxtaposed with the debauchery of the previous night's party. I felt a reverence for what that man and child were doing, unlike the vague embarrassment for our behavior the previous night—all the drugs and non-island people acting

66

proprietary about the luau.

As the sun came up over the mountain, the grandfather and grandson folded their net and disappeared into the thick foliage bordering the beach, like ghosts, and I felt as if I'd been privy to some sacred ancestral custom.

We stayed on for a few days at the house, romping in the surf, flirting with all the girls, getting used to island time. A neighborhood woman offered us a lift to the airport one morning so we took it. She had her child with her, a four-year-old girl, who rode in the front with her mother while Greg, our friend and I sat squashed in the back, grateful for a ride. Our sleeping bags and backpacks and surfboards stuck out of her small trunk. The woman was nostalgic that day, and she drove all the way around the island, giving us a commentary on geography and history of the places we saw.

It was late afternoon by the time we landed in Wailuku, on the island of Maui. The first order of business was to purchase a car. We stored our possessions at the airport, hitched into town, and began negotiations at the first car lot we came to. An old Chinese man owned the used car lot, and he drove a hard bargain, but finally we bought a '46 Plymouth convertible for forty-five dollars. Each of us put in fifteen dollars for our share. Minimum wage at that time was two dollars an hour. Still, the car was a junker. It burned oil but we figured it would last the summer. It was green with a black convertible top, which we immediately put down. We drove the "new" car back to the airport, retrieved our things, and began the long drive to the other side of the island, where the surf was.

About forty-five minutes later we stopped at the first surf spot we could see from the road. Maalaea. The trade

67

winds rustled the palms overlooking the surf spot, and the waves seemed to go on forever, and were large, how large we couldn't tell because nobody was out in the water. After a time we left. The car was hard to start, but finally did, though it would not go very fast. About five miles from Lahaina the rings seized up, stopping our car right in the road. Dead in the water. It took quite an effort to get the car off the road—there were very few cars going in either direction, still, we didn't wish to abandon it where it died, causing an accident. By the time we did get it pushed onto the shoulder, we were hot and disappointed. For some reason we began stoning that car. Bashing the tires and body with rocks. We had the good sense not to break the windshield, though it was tempting. All the other windows were rolled down or they would have been fair game.

While we stoned the car, a station wagon full of Australian surfers stopped in the road.

Doin mates? the driver said.

We told them our story. A few of the younger guys got out and threw rocks at the car with us. Then we piled into the already full car, with all our things, for the rest of the trip to Lahaina. Once in town, we hooked up with a surfer from Huntington Beach, a soon-to-be famous surfer that Greg knew very well. We stored our things behind their house, and the soon-to-be famous surfer's wife did our laundry and fed us, and tended the baby boy she had with the soon to be famous surfer. The whole family was profiled in *Esquire* recently, when the now-famous surfer's son, all grown up, was the hook of the article.

We'd surf Lahaina in the mornings, then forage for food. In the afternoons we'd drive to different surf spots with people who had cars. If nobody had room, we'd surf Lahaina some more.

At some point we met a guy who was bodysurfing his way around the world. He was an older guy who had nowhere to stay. We got someone to tow our car to the abandoned library on the south edge of town, and the bodysurfer moved into it, sort of like an apartment or something. He could lock his things in the trunk. He put up the roof and had a dry place to sleep when it rained at night. He really liked that car.

We ran into another guy from Huntington Beach who lived out at Kihei. He invited us along, so we hitchhiked to the country—what the islanders called it, though for my money everything was country. A drunken man, a really drunk man, picked us up. He was going all the way to Makena. We didn't think we'd ever see Kihei—this guy was weaving and slurring his words, and trying to carry on a conversation as he "drove." He was a sailor from W.W. II who'd never returned to the mainland. He sang the praises of island women—he'd married one, I'd gathered—and told us his war stories. We got out at the park in Kihei, and watched the guy swerve on his way. The good news was that there were few cars on the road.

The park at Kihei overlooks the surf, and there was a gathering going on. I immediately saw a guy I knew from Seal Beach, the younger brother of a friend of mine who'd died on his graduation night, the year before my own. The younger brother took us over to a cooler loaded with beer and told us to have some. As I took a beer, I felt myself being lifted off the ground. By my neck. A three-hundred pound Samoan said, Why you takum beer, haole boy? in the singsong pidgen English the islanders speak.

Neither the younger brother, Greg, nor anybody else I knew was nearby. I apologized to the Brobdingnagian islander; we negotiated for a time but when I tried to return the beer to the cooler he wouldn't hear of it. That Samoan taught me a lesson about humility that afternoon on the beach in Kihei, and I drank numerous beers with him and his friends.

Sometime before sunset we made for the house of our friend, which was down the beach from the park. Our friend was living with his friends who were older than we were. And also: they were selling drugs. Big time. They didn't want to know us, so we slept on the beach in Kihei, with the most stars in the sky you'll ever see, except maybe way down in Baja California, you'll view something similar. We stayed on the beach, surfing every day, hanging out with our friend, staying out of the way of the drug dealers.

When the drug dealers were leaving the island for good they wanted to sell their car quickly. A really solid fifty-four Chevy, all green. If we'd take them to the airport, they said, we could have their car for one-hundred and fifty dollars. Greg and I split the cost, which took most of our money, but we really wanted the mobility.

The car ran great, and after we dropped off the drug dealers, this overwhelming sense of freedom overtook me. For some reason I was driving. Greg was sitting shotgun. On the way back to Lahaina a police cruiser pulled me over. I was arrested for driving without a Hawaiian driver's license. They also thought I was a drug dealer, they told me later at the police station, where I'd been taken. They finally believed my story when I produced a bill of sale, which I'd procured from the drug dealers, something my father had instilled in me. Always get a bill of sale, my father had told me, especially for a big item such as a car.

After my arrest I got a Hawaiian driver's license, and our lives settled down into a nice pattern: surf all we wanted anywhere we wanted, sleep on different beaches, and sightsee in the afternoons after the wind picked up.

One problem we were having was that our money was running low, what with the purchase of two cars. So Greg had been fortunate to get a part-time job at the Kaanapali Resort. It was on the way to drop off Greg at his job that we first saw Pee Wee, Makao, and Donna. They were hitchhiking. We pulled over and gave them a lift.

Pee Wee was short, dark and solidly built; the phrase "brick shithouse" comes to mind when I think of Pee Wee's body. Makao had that almost kinky hair that some Hawaiians have, plus a regal, distracted air, and an incredible lean, wiry strength. Donna was young, a beautiful Hawaiian girl, slightly taller than Pee Wee, and obviously his girlfriend. They had just flown over from Oahu, from Waikiki, the Jungle, more accurately, where they lived.

With the exception of Donna, we would remain together the rest of our stay on Maui.

We dropped Greg off that afternoon at Kaanapali, and I took our "guests" to the beach where we were currently sleeping, just up the road from Mala Wharf. We made camp in the dusk, lighting a fire, and talking until it was time to pick up Greg, after ten o'clock. We slept late the next morning.

Until the sun would come over the hills, that is, for it would be too hot to be in your sleeping bag any longer, and the insects would be moving, so you'd just walk the thirty steps to the sea and get in. Cool ocean water first thing in the morning, every morning. Then you'd decide where you'd surf.

Since there was a "woman" with us—Donna must have been seventeen—we were all on our best chivalrous behavior. Which meant we'd do more than the usual sightseeing. We drove out to the lava beds at Makena, and we drove to the Seven Sacred Falls over in Hana, in the rain forest. We drove up to Haleakala Crater, where you can see clouds materialize before your eyes, and where there are plants that only exist in that crater, out of the entire world. Once we even went to Wailuku, the largest town on the island, to have a look around.

After the trip to the Seven Sacred Falls, Pee Wee and Makao pooled their money and purchased a ticket back to Oahu for Donna. Money was now too tight to have Donna going without, I supposed, thus she was sent home. I was half right in this regard. We dropped her off at the airport in Wailuku, and she was genuinely sad to leave us, hugging Greg and me and Makao all at once for a long time. She kissed Pee Wee good-bye, and I think she cried as she boarded her plane, though I'm not sure, as she never looked back at us.

Pee Wee and Makao were completely out of money. Greg and I were down to nothing as well, though we did have Greg's tip money, and he was now bringing back scraps of food, which Pee Wee, Makao, and I would split late at night, sometimes all we'd get for dinner. I learned a lot about the islands from Pee Wee and Makao on those long nights when we'd sit before our fire on the beach, Greg gone working.

They told me about the island myths, and of the Menehunes, the island spirits that set things right. They also told me of their lives in Honolulu's "jungle," where they had grown up. The equivalent of East L.A., or Watts, I figured, a place where poor Hawaiians lived, people who were darker than the newer arrivals and who were passed over by newcomers with money and status, and in all probability lighter skinned.

My skin coloring is olive but I was now so dark from the relentless Hawaiian summer sun that I could pass for a local, something I liked.

On those nights we talked, Makao told me of his imprisonment for armed robbery, for which he'd recently been released, and how he'd spent over half his twenty-five years of life locked up. Pee Wee was an orphan, flitting between lousy foster homes his entire life, until he was fifteen, when he'd gone out on his own, and had been ever since. Makao liked to sniff gasoline, which he'd try to siphon from our car when we weren't watching. I still have this image of him sitting on the darkened beach, high on gasoline, strumming his ukulele telling us ghost stories, or things that had happened while he was incarcerated.

♦

Our routine was permanently changed the day Pee Wee and Makao borrowed our car. They were gone all day, and into the evening, and Greg and I began to wonder if we'd ever see them again. Greg and I stayed on the beach all day—he didn't work that night. We talked about how hard

73

it was getting, what with no money and no place over our heads, and we talked about our promise to return to attend school. We got the bright idea to check out community colleges on Maui. The word college was a mantra in my house while I was growing up. It was assumed by my parents that all their children would attend. I had wanted to go to UC Irvine, the new college right in my backyard, but was turned down, and this sort of took the wind out of my college sails. But still, a promise is a promise, and I'd promised my parents I'd attend college in autumn.

As it got later and later, the thought crossed our minds that possibly Pee Wee and Makao really weren't coming back. Had taken off with our car. However, they did return, quite late, and wouldn't talk about where they'd been. And they had all kinds of food with them.

The next morning we feasted on their "catch." In my naïveté, it took me some time to put two and two together. Greg and Pee Wee were out surfing—since Pee Wee and Makao didn't have boards, they'd use ours, and we'd surf in pairs. Makao asked to use the car again tonight. I asked him for what reason. He wouldn't tell me. I asked him where he'd gotten the money to buy all the food we now had. He remained silent. I too remained silent, watching the surf break before us. I don't want to be responsible for your stealing, I told Makao. He wouldn't look at me. Don't steal for me anymore, I told him. He smiled at me, that smile with his dimples. It was an odd contradiction, this really rugged, handsome Hawaiian man, covered with tattoos, smiling at me, his dimples showing. I felt very safe in Makao's presence.

When Greg and Pee Wee came in from surfing, we decid-

74

ed to drive into Lahaina to see if the bay was breaking. On the drive over to Lahaina, Pee Wee and Makao began working on Greg and me, asking to borrow the car again. We wanted to know what they were up to. They refused to tell us. We were at an impasse on the issue. They were insistent upon using the car, though they wouldn't tell us for what purpose. We were equally insistent about not lending the car to them unless they told us what they were going to do. Both of them began sulking a bit, so Greg and I went out on our boards in Lahaina Bay.

Lahaina is a nineteenth century whaling town, small, and charming, in the 1970s it was at any rate. The main street is behind a long sea wall. There's a grassy park leading out to a point. The white clapboard hotel with verandahs all the way around it is before the point. At anchor in the bay and close to the point is an old whaling schooner. It's like a museum in that it is a throwback to how the town must have looked when whaling was a staple for an entire fleet of ships.

Out in the water Greg saw a guy he worked with, who told him he was needed at work tonight, his night off. Greg didn't mind working, and I was secretly glad, for this now made the car issue a moot one.

That night while Greg was at work we didn't build a fire on the beach, we just lay there on top of our sleeping bags watching the night sky, listening to the surf break on the coral reef. Something had changed, some barrier forever up, some trust broken. We didn't speak much either, the still and dark night a metaphor for the mood that had overtaken us.

Sometime late, before Greg had returned from work, as

we lay there dozing, we saw lights on the beach. The lights were heading our way, getting closer. After a time we could see that the lights were from torches, but we couldn't see the people who carried them. Makao got all worked up and began speaking in Hawaiian to Pee Wee. Pee Wee told me the Menehunes were out tonight.

Should we leave? I said.

You can't get away, Makao said.

So we stood our ground, prone in the sand, hoping the spirits wouldn't notice us.

When the torches were close enough to illuminate their bearers, we could see that these were people, not spirits, and they were islanders, though there were a few whites at the back. Makao was still worked up.

The procession had the effect of a truth serum on Makao. Later that night he told me why they wanted to use our car. They were going to do a "job." Checking it out was where they had been the previous night. Casing it. I told them no way, they couldn't use the car for a robbery. They didn't understand my negative attitude toward their plan. It was on the other side of the island, they reasoned.

I don't want you to get caught, I told them.

We won't get caught, Pee Wee said.

I don't want you to go to jail, I said. I won't be a part of that. Besides, if you use our car, then we're involved too. Greg and I are involved.

They listened to this, then let the matter die; however, I knew the wheels of their plan were still in motion.

The next day Greg and I used his tip money to buy gas so we could drive to Wailuku, where the community college was located. We talked with a counselor who told us that we could still sign up, but we'd have to pay out-of-state tuition. We couldn't even afford the resident's tuition, much less the higher cost of out-of-state tuition. That was that. We'd have to forego college or return home in order to attend.

There was, of course, that other matter of war. You could get a deferment by being in college. I'd wanted to go to college, but not community college. I wanted to attend university. Greg didn't care about college one way or the other. Neither of us wished to be drafted. We'd have to return home.

That evening we watched the sunset at the sea wall. We told Pee Wee and Makao our intention to leave the island. The sun was almost down, the water oily slick with a cream coloring where the sun reflected off it.

What's the matter, can't take it? Makao said.

You know like us no mo? Pee Wee said. Too good for us?

The place no good fo you, bro? Makao said to me. He punched me hard in the arm, a prelude, I was sure, to throwing blows.

I didn't want to fight him, for he was tough as nails, I was sure. Pee Wee had herded Greg away from Makao and me. If Makao was going to kick my ass after everything we'd been through, after all the things I'd done for him, fine. But I was going to hit back, that was for sure.

You too good for me, haole boy? Makao had never called me a haole before, possibly in deference to my skin coloring, which wasn't all that different from his. Haole is a racial epithet, slung at foreigners by Hawaiians. I'd heard a Hawaiian once say to a newly arrived mainlander, You likum beef, haole boy? The guy, who was very white, not yet tanned, said, Yeah, I eat meat. The Hawaiian punched the white guy in the face a number of times. Beef meant fight. Haole boy was a racial pejorative, equivalent to calling someone from the South a "cracker."

I'm going to college, I said to Makao. I sunk my center of gravity, tensed my stomach, and gritted my teeth with my tongue in back, the way my father had taught me.

College? Pee Wee said from over by Greg.

Yeah, Greg said.

I promised, I said.

Makao dropped his arms. He relaxed. He smiled. The sun was down. That's hard, he said. That's good.

We spent the evening under the world's largest banyan tree, or so the sign claimed, drinking beer, listening to Makao sing and strum his ukulele. Both Pee Wee and Makao encouraged Greg and me to finish college, to get degrees.

We sold the car and gave them some money, though not as much as we wanted to: They wouldn't take it. We gave them the key to the '46 Plymouth, the one that had broken down in another lifetime, so they'd have a place to lock up their things. We took our good-byes, and I never saw them again.

I sometimes think about Pee Wee and Makao. I always had a plane ticket to fall back onto. I was going to live with my parents and go to college. Pee Wee and Makao were going back to the "jungle" when they were finished on Maui.

MEXICANS DON'T SKI

IF YOU HAD ON YOUR SKI BOOTS, your skis waxed and ready, and you knew who was loading the gondola, you could ride to the top of the mountain, ski down, and be back to work by the end of your lunch break. Thirty minutes for lunch, when working in the rental shop. The gondola took twenty-two minutes. You'd return to work while still in your ski boots, however, if it was busy, and it was on the weekends, for sure. It was a precision drill, that, skiing down the face of the cornice, down the backside of Chair 3, all the way down the whole of Mammoth Mountain in eight minutes. But it could be done. And I did it numerous times that winter I lived in the mountains. The guy loading the gondola had to let you on immediately, though. Because in those days, on a weekend, the wait to get on the gondola was over one hour. But since you were an employee, they'd give you a break. Rhubarb was the boss of the rental and ski repair shops. He was a great skier, a former ski school muck-a-muck, and still taught private lessons. He supported the exuberance of young skiers.

In the writing program I attended many years later, I wrote about my skiing experiences. One of the professors who ran the workshop said, Mexicans don't ski. A disgruntled student who was in the process of filing a sexual harassment charge against the same professor, pressured me to file a racial harassment charge against him for the comment. I refused her request. There weren't a lot of "Mexicans" skiing. Not at Mammoth Mountain, anyway. Maybe in Chile there are. But the professor also meant this: What I was writing about wasn't often written in fiction. A Chicano skier.

After my Hawaii trip I did keep my word. I enrolled in the community college literally across the street from my childhood home. As I look back now I can see that I was depressed. Depressed that I wasn't in a school that offered me more of a challenge. The teachers were fine at the community college. Many of the students didn't wish to be there, however. That sort of dragged everything down. I would get the highest test scores in the forum classes, and I'd stay out late at night, sleeping in in the mornings. I'd sold my car so I couldn't even go surfing. I'd walk to school.

One weekend in November I went skiing at Mammoth Mountain. There were a bunch of guys from my high school, guys who were older than I, but still, I knew them, and they all lived in a house trailer. I decided I'd rather ski than attend community college. So when the semester was finished, I moved up to the mountains. This was the winter of '69, a fierce and powerful winter, and the main road to Mammoth was closed—U.S. 395. So I had to go up to Lake Tahoe, on the front side of the Sierras, the Pacific side. When there was a break in the weather I dropped down to Mammoth.

My high school acquaintances let me stay at the trailer; around town it was called the Psychedelic Trailer. It was a thirty foot, single-width house trailer with two bedrooms.

The bedrooms were occupied by Ronny and Dean. Danny, the guy I knew best, and another guy named Desi, slept in the living room. I too would sleep in the living room on the floor. But I'd be skiing.

Danny got me a job in the rental shop right away, where the rest of the guys worked, except for Ronny and Dean who worked in the more glamorous repair shop, ergo they had their own bedrooms. We'd work all weekend—that was why you'd only have the lunch break to ski—and then work another full day, two half days, and the rest of the time was for skiing. You got free lift tickets, and you got food at half price.

So my days were filled with work and skiing. My nights were spent at the Psychedelic Trailer, drinking red wine with snow in it—wine snowcones. Some of the guys got really loaded. They painted the ceilings with black phosphorescent paint and hung up the Starship Enterprise and the Klingon warship whose name I don't know. They'd take acid and watch those space ships twirling in the black glowing sky. While outside the winter raged on.

Desi had been in Vietnam, and no matter how much we tried to trip him up, no matter how loaded he was or how much we offered him bribes, he wouldn't tell of his war experiences. He'd been in Cambodia, he said, with Special Forces, and had sworn an oath of secrecy. And he kept his oath. Desi did.

After a time of sleeping on a trailer floor, sharing a trailer with five other guys, unable to read, to do anything—you were never alone—I moved out to Old Mammoth. With another older guy I knew named Turtle. He was from Huntington Beach, and my older brother's age. Turtle let me live in the trailer he rented but never stayed at, and so for twenty-five dollars a month I virtually had my own place. It was a small trailer, fifteen feet, and it was entirely buried in snow. We dug a chute to slide down into the entry. But after the Psychedelic Trailer, my solitude was sublime. I wandered around on snowshoes out at the Meadows, and heard the noisiest quiet you could ever imagine. An ice blue day with no wind and no birds and no sounds from the trees rustling and no people. Just silence and snow. A roaring silence, a standing up on its hindlegs and bellowing silence.

Turtle got me a part-time job where he worked. He was the cook at the Arlburg Chalet Inn, a steakhouse. I bused tables on the weekend nights. It was a cool scene. Turtle was the cook, as I said, and a guy named Dennis was the waiter, I was the busboy, and a guy named Jesse was the dishwasher. Turtle and Dennis were late twenties, I was late teens, Jesse was late forties.

Jesse was short with thick black hair and his real name was Jésus, but he went by the more American-friendly Jesse. My older brother's middle name was Jess, a diminutive of Jésus. Jesse was dark, even in the throes of a Mammoth Mountain winter. He, a woman who worked in the ski shop named Madeline, and I were the only Chicanos on the mountain that I knew of. Jesse spoke with an accent. Madeline and I didn't. Madeline lived with a guy I skied with, and she gave us great discounts on equipment at the ski shop. Where I bought my Rosignol skis, my poles, my boots, my down parka, my powder pants, my gloves, everything. When I first arrived at Mammoth, the only things I had were ski pants my mother had made, a sweater she'd knitted for me, and oiled work boots. Madeline got me into thermal boots right away.

Jesse taught me how to wait tables.

I'd already worked in a restaurant when in high school. A place called El Toro. On the bluff above Sunset Beach, between Seal Beach and Huntington Beach, the only Mexican restaurant around in those days. Now, of course, they're everywhere. My friend Jim P got me the job at El Toro. My friend who died on his graduation night, after we'd surfed at Trestles all day. When I called him the next morning to go surfing, I had to hear his mother crying, telling me he'd been killed. But Jim got me the job. The A's owned the restaurant. Mary, the matriarch, was Mexican, and she wanted a brown front man, so I didn't bus tables for very long—I began taking names for the waiting list. They tried to tell me I was the maitre d' but I knew shit about the restaurant business. Mary did tell me, however, that if people wished to slip me money so they didn't have to wait so long, I could take it.

But that was the extent of my restaurant experience: a short time busing tables and a glorified receptionist.

After a time busing tables at the Arlburg I told Dennis that I wanted to wait tables. He told me he'd teach me. But the only thing he showed me how to do was to fold linen napkins into a bird of paradise shape, and how to set a place, which was busing, after all.

Sometimes when Jesse would get backed up on the dishwashing I'd help him. Once when he couldn't show for work I covered for him. Dishwashing sucked. You were all wet for hours, and the stench drove me nuts, which was why Jesse always had the door to the tiny kitchen open, letting in the frigid night mountain air, but better than the musty air from the restaurant. After the time I filled in for Jesse, he told me he'd show me how to wait tables.

Nobody believed that he'd been a waiter, but I did. He was a far better waiter than Dennis. Except Dennis was over six feet tall, a pure bullshit artist, and a decent waiter. Jesse was maybe five feet four, had thick black hair, and dark Indian skin, and spoke with a thick accent. The skiers weren't going to let him serve them, he reasoned. And Nick, the owner of the restaurant evidently agreed, for Jesse couldn't even bus tables, as I did. So he remained in the back, out of sight, washing dishes. And teaching me how to wait tables.

Jesse loved the craft he no longer plied, I could tell. For in that tiny kitchen, where there was barely enough room to turn around, he showed me how to uncork a bottle of fine wine, how to open a linen napkin with a flourish before placing it before the diner, how to load plates on your arm, the way in which you write down an order so you don't have to ask who gets what. Jesse was patient with me, laughed with me at my errors, and I want to say we two were sort of a reverse Pygmalion, except Jesse wasn't in love with his creation: me; he was in love with his craft. The artist wasn't in love with the art object, the artist was in love with the process, which in Jesse's case, he couldn't perform.

And I got good, serving salads with aplomb, bullshiting with the patrons about how the skiing was that day (something I had over Dennis since he didn't ski, but claimed he did), or advising them which wax to use the following day.

Dennis, it seemed, got jealous. He cut me back from

Thursday, Friday, Saturday and Sunday nights to just Saturday night. I didn't give a shit; I didn't need the money. I had the job at the lifts working in the rental shop. I skied free. Hell, I was banking all sorts of money.

Some time prior, I'd had to move out of the trailer at Old Mammoth. Turtle, it seemed, was taking my share of the rent but wasn't actually paying rent. Or so the owner of the trailer told me one afternoon when I returned to find Turtle's possessions on a toboggan in the snow, about to be transported away. I told the owner my story, and he believed me, and let me get my meager things.

I confronted Turtle about this. He laughed and said he didn't care about any of that shit anyway. He said I could stay with him rent-free. He had a room at the Fun House, as the dorms were called, where the Arlburg workers lived. So I began living there, eating across the street at night at the Arlburg—Nick, the owner, made huge pots of something every night for his employees to eat. I worked and skied during the days. At night I bused tables or hung out in the Arlburg's disco, the only place around that had live music. The reason I hung out there was because they had all the Olympic footage of Jean Claude Killey's slalom, giant slalom, and downhill runs, the year he won three gold medals. I studied those films while the light show blasted and the bar band crashed, and Turtle and Dennis picked up women. The good news was that Turtle was seldom in his room—he was a real alley cat, a different woman every night. Probably something to do with the breakup of his marriage, he said.

And so the winter moved forward, huge storms battering the resort, closing it down at times. The winter that the ski patrolman named Charlie was lost at the beginning of a three day storm. But he dug in, and waited, and he survived, a truly good sign. On the days the lifts were closed I'd shovel snow for five dollars an hour, cash. I was banking all kinds of money, what with two jobs and cash on the side. I didn't have a girlfriend, and if you did go on a date, you'd probably go with her to somebody's house for a dinner or a party.

Just before spring was on the horizon, a guy from my high school named Dan B showed up. He was trouble. He was the guy who'd fought Steve I on sight their senior year. They'd torn up a Denny's restaurant one time in Seal Beach when they'd crossed paths and duked it out. They were both arrested. Anytime at school when they crossed paths, they fought. The problem was there was no clear winner. So they kept fighting. After Steve I graduated—he was two years older than I—he enlisted in the Army and did two tours of duty in Vietnam. Steve was instrumental in my own decision not to fight in that war, for he'd said, Don't go, no matter what, don't go. And he was a decorated soldier. Desi was a bit more ambivalent about it. He thought you served your country no matter what, though he couldn't point out any good he'd done over there.

After Dan B graduated he spent time in a Mexican jail, or so I'd heard. For pot, I'd heard. But still, he would openly smoke joints on the streets of Mammoth Lakes. Anywhere he pleased. That was the sort of person he was. A big guy. A guy who could hold his own with Steve I.

Dan B got a job at the lifts, though in what capacity I couldn't tell you. On his days off he'd go down to the flatlands, what the locals called anywhere that wasn't in the mountains, and he'd score drugs. Pot and acid and downers.

I knew him from high school, was on good terms with him, even skied with him a few times, though he was too large to be any good skiing.

So when he came to me to tell me that he was going to kill Turtle, I took the threat seriously. Dan B claimed that Turtle had stolen a jar of downers from him. I told him that couldn't be so. I didn't know Turtle that well, still he didn't strike me as someone who would steal someone else's drugs. I wasn't remembering the rent fiasco.

When next I saw Turtle I told him about Dan B's threat. He shook his head in disbelief and called Dan B an asshole. They didn't cross paths, I suppose, because there wasn't a fight, which I'd expected.

No, the thing you don't expect is the thing that goes down.

I never dreamed Jesse would be in a fight. Kind, sweet Jesse. The man who'd cared enough to show me how to wait tables. It wasn't a fight in the true sense. It was a whipping. An ass-kicking. Jesse's face was all swollen and his eyes were puffy and black and his lip was huge and split. And he wouldn't talk about it. And he withdrew into himself after his beating. No longer cared to show me the finer points of restaurant work. Stopped talking altogether, really.

From what I could find out Jesse was beaten because he was short and dark and Mexican. What we'd now call a hate crime. Seems he'd gone out for a drink after work one night and he'd tried to talk with a woman. Some one there didn't take kindly to that. And Jessie was beaten, right there in the bar.

Dan B kept at me as well, saying that Turtle had taken his drugs, but I'd insist that he hadn't. One night Turtle finally admitted to me that, yes, he had taken the jar of downers. Had followed Dan B and had watched him bury the drugs, and gone back and taken them. He thought it was funny.

I moved out of the Fun House, got away from Turtle. Quit my job busing tables as well. Jesse wanted nothing to do with anybody. I began hanging out with new friends, guys who only wanted to ski, and ski well. I was becoming pretty good. I did, after all, have a background in surfing, and skiing was just like surfing except the "water" was frozen.

And I worked hard at my job at the lifts in the rental shop. Soon they put me in charge of the cash register, the plum job. Much better than adjusting boots and bindings hour after hour. I also got to set my own schedule. Other than working the register when it was busy. So now I was skiing seven days a week. And I was in charge of the older guys from my high school who'd worked there longer than I. They didn't like this one bit.

Toward the end of winter a guy named Rick T, who also just happened to be from Seal Beach, and was a manager, had some T-shirts made up. They said: I survived the winter of '69. Those shirts were cool and there were only so many of them and I wanted one. Rick T gave me one. He also told me that Rhubarb and Vic L, the two guys in charge of the department I worked in, had recommended me for Rhubarb's job. Vic was quitting, Rhubarb was moving up to Vic's job, and I could have the job running both the rental shop and repair shop, if I wanted. It was a year-round position, a salaried one.

When word of this got out my former "friends" from Huntington Beach were openly hostile toward me. I had to exert my authority when giving them orders, no matter how uncomfortable I was in that capacity.

When Turtle heard about the job offer he told me Rick T and I would be the only ones left on the mountain, the only ones up there for the summer. The Dan B thing had blown over when Dan B was arrested for drug possession.

I had terrible cabin fever. The snow gets to you after a winter. So much that I used to hitchhike down to Bishop to watch the spring night baseball games. It felt as if we'd entered a new land, a land without snow.

I didn't take that job. I don't know if it was because of the lonely sound the wind made when blowing over the dirty snow at the side of the road after almost everyone had left the resort. Or if it was because when I'd see Jesse he'd barely acknowledge the fact that we knew each other.

A few years later, on Mt. Hood in Oregon, I took the ski instructor's test, which I passed, though I never taught.

RACIAL POLITICS AND HOBIE CATS

IN THOSE DAYS you just went to the Parks and Recreation Dept. to sign up for a class. I don't know if the same is true today or not. But that was how it was done in Newport Beach. I lived in Corona del Mar, which is part of Newport Beach, ergo I could take classes offered by the city. And I did. Beginning Sailing, Hobie 14s. Fourteen foot long catamarans. You had to pass a swimming test, though, and that was it. You could sail.

Richie M was the instructor. We sat on the sand—all the students who ranged in age from late adolescence to middle age, more women than men—listening to Richie talk about sailing. The morning was warm, and the small breeze rustled the halyards so they clanked against the masts of the sailboats lined up on the beach. The sky was filled with blue possibility.

Richie said: Sailing is a misnomer. It really should be called sucking. That's how the wind propels the boat forward. The wind hits the sail, creates a vacuum behind it, which moves the boat forward. By sucking. What Richie M said.

Now I'm able to see the reality of the physical nature of sailing. And it does make for an interesting play on words. Let's go sucking. But imagine Ahab sucking after Moby

Dick. It doesn't work, no romance in it. Therefore sailing. As opposed to sucking.

After an introductory lecture, in which Richie explained some terms and showed us the parts of a catamaran, we were told to drive to the other side of the bay, where the city had a pool. For the swim test. You had to be able to tread water for ten minutes.

No sweat for me. I grew up surfing. When in college I learned how to swim in a pool, doing flip turns, breathing, and numerous strokes besides the crawl. In fact I swam on a daily basis in those days, when I had a membership at the Y, the one overlooking the Back Bay. In those days I was twenty-six. I built houses for money. After working hard physically for eight hours, I swam or body surfed, this after a three-to-five-mile jog. Treading water for ten minutes was not a problem.

A few of the students couldn't pass the swim test, however. They were encouraged to take a swim class but would not be allowed in the sailing class. Next week we would sail.

About Richie. He was a good-looking man. And in retrospect I can see that one of the reasons there were so many women in the class was his presence. Maybe the word was out. He was about six four with a boyish face, anywhere from twenty-five to twenty-eight-years old. He had light blue eyes and that sea-crusty hair that guys who make their living on the water have, as well as a peeled nose. He was in good shape, though certainly not what we now call "buff." No weights for Richie. Just sailing and sex, I learned later. His regimen for good health.

As for me, I was coming off a long relationship. After my skiing days, I returned to college. But I wished to attend a school where I could ski. My two choices in the West were Colorado or Oregon. I opted for Oregon, since I'd made a trip up there and had loved it. My father loaned me his car, and I drove up at the end of summer, got a job on Mt. Hood at the lifts, and registered for school. I'd go to state university in Portland. Where, in a volleyball class, I met the woman with whom I'd share a number of years of my life. We lived together. After our breakup I was sort of out of it. And supposedly looking...because you can't remain in a shell forever, there's more than one fish in the sea, time will take care of it, you're young, you're supposed to be with many people. Etcetera.

And let me tell you, there were women around Richie. Beautiful women. And Richie was just himself. No airs, no pretenses, no bullshit. If he wanted to date someone he said so. No flirtatious mating dance hooey. And this. The women made it so obvious if they were interested.

The following week was consumed, as usual, in work and exercise. I knew there were classes offered in the afternoons at the city docks so I went down to the bay to watch people sail, to watch Richie teach. The first afternoon there was an advanced catamaran class which Richie pretty much left alone. The second afternoon, a Thursday, I was taken aback. Richie was loading what at that time were called mongoloid idiots and are now called children with Down's syndrome on to an 18' Sol Cat. The trampoline was much larger than the fourteen foot Hobie I'd be sailing, and the boat was riding low in the water, for all its precious cargo, and even though I didn't know Richie well at that time, I sensed that he was truly happy. He was surrounded by adoring kids, and he tooled them around the bay ever so gently, and the kids shrieked with delight as they made pass after pass in front of the beach where the sailing classes were based.

Sailing on those Saturday mornings was a blast. You could just forget everything about your life and exist in the present moment: Were you sheeted in properly? Were you too close to the mooring cans in the bay, where the boats would drift? Were you balanced correctly so that you could react should your pontoon come out of the water? Stuff like that, stuff that made you be *there*. And of course this was when the class changed. Because the adventurous ones began riding up on one pontoon. So Richie decreed it was time for the weaning process.

Those early weeks we sailed Richie was either on the boat with us or close on his sixteen foot Hobie cat. Now that we were ready for the weaning process, Richie said, we'd work on capsizing our boats the following week. You will capsize, Richie said.

I still worked all week, still went down to the bay a few times to watch the advanced classes. Richie taught full-time for the City of Newport Beach. He had classes in the mornings and afternoons. He taught classes on the weekends as well. He now recognized me but we weren't friends or anything.

This one afternoon I stayed until sunset, until the class was over and all the students had dragged the cats up to the wall where they were stored. The students had left and I saw Richie dragging his larger boat up to the wall. Without communicating, I began to help him. It was far easier for two guys to haul his boat over the sand. And I suppose that night, with the ferry's horn blaring as it brought cars to Balboa Island, as the dark slick waters of Newport Bay glistened in the sunset, we locked in our short friendship as I helped him pull the thick chain through the boats, padlock them, and hide the key.

The next weekend, in late June, was overcast with a stiff south wind blowing. Even though the area has mild weather, any deviation from it seems extreme. June is often overcast and drizzly in the mornings, and then a sort of hazy warmth envelopes the coastline in the afternoon. Except when a south wind blows. When a south wind blows oftentimes it will stay cloudy all day, even rain. The wind, coupled with the cold water of the bay—fifty-five degrees—made for an ill-boding capsizing lesson.

This was the drill: Everyone would sail a Hobie 14 out to the middle of the bay. Richie would be next to you on his sixteen footer. If you couldn't capsize your boat he'd help you get the mast over. We watched from shore as Richie went out with the first sailors. Things went pretty well, except for a woman who had trouble getting her boat over. Richie helped her. Other than that, everything was as he'd explained it to us.

Then came my turn. I sailed the Hobie out to the middle of the bay, turned it over, and went through the procedure. First I unsheeted the mainsail so the boat could be maneuvered into the wind. Then with the righting line I put the mast directly into the wind. I swam around to the lee of the boat where I sheeted in the mainsail, and pulled the righting line over the pontoon that was up. All I had to do, in theory, was get the mainsail up enough to get wind under it. The wind would do the work of righting the boat. Piece of cake. We'd all practiced the moves in shallow water. I felt no qualms. I was a strong swimmer, in good shape, and knew the dynamics of getting the boat over and back up.

Except I didn't plan for a big gust of wind at the same precise time that I tugged on the righting line. This is what happened: Not only did the boat come up, it came all the way over on top of me with such force that the mast went underwater. I broke the surface, colder now, and untangled myself from the lines.

Richie was smiling. That was quite a pull, he said.

What happened? I said.

You're turtled, he said.

What's that mean?

Your mast is underwater. Not the end of the world, but not what you want to happen. You've got to get the mast up, he said.

How do I do that?

Same principle, Richie said. Get on the lee pontoon, pull the righting line over the windward pontoon, and get it up enough so the wind helps you right the boat.

It sounded good, but when I did as instructed, nothing. I told Richie that the mast was stuck in the mud. It felt that heavy to me.

Not so, Richie calmly said. You're in deep water.

Okay, I thought, I'll make an effort and then Richie will get in and help me. I tugged a few times. Nothing.

Do it like you want it to happen, Richie said.

The wind had picked up. My teeth were chattering. The bay was not the least inviting, not the way it was on those other Saturdays, or on those evenings when I'd come down and take off my shirt at seven o'clock. It was dark overcast and small whitecaps formed all around us.

95

C'mon, Richie said, you can do it.

We were almost to the other side of the bay. I saw my classmates, little and huddled together, far away on the opposite shore, and I wondered, Why was Richie doing this to me? I thought he liked me. I thought he'd help me.

I'll tow you back out to the middle, he said. Get on the pontoon.

I took hold of the pontoon, gave Richie the righting line, and he sheeted in his sixteen, pulling us back into deeper water and away from the moored boats tied to the mooring cans.

Once again I began pulling on the righting line, hoping that the boat would miraculously right itself. Once again in a slow dance the wind blew us down and across the bay. A few sailors came right up to Richie, telling him to help me.

We're conducting a class, Richie told them. Everything's under control.

Most people sailed in long pants and windbreakers or sweatshirts. Those sailing cats wore wetsuits. I wore swim trunks. I was cold. And getting pissed.

I don't know that I can do it, I said to Richie.

Nobody's going to help you, if that's what you think, he said. When you're at sea nobody will ever help you. You've got to do it yourself, he said. You've got to depend on yourself and no one else, Richie said.

I was getting scared. And tired. Cold and losing my concentration. Again we blew against the mooring cans at the far side of the bay.

As Richie was about to pull me back out to the middle of the bay, a guy motored up in one of those restored launches like you see at the Balboa Bay Club.

What's going on? the guy said.

A class, Richie said.

This guy's been in the water about forty minutes, the guy in the launch said.

All right, I thought, finally someone sticking up for me.

You're interfering with a class, sir, Richie said.

Help him out of the water, the guy in the launch said.

Can't do that, Richie said. He's got to do it himself.

Get him out of the water now, the guy in the launch said.

I was sure they could hear my teeth chattering.

Richie shook his head.

I'll come aboard and make you, the guy in the launch said.

You could tell he was used to giving orders, and to having his orders followed.

That's your choice, sir, Richie said. If you want to try, you're certainly welcome. Richie stood up to his full height on the boat's trampoline.

Some other sailors had gathered around, watching the showdown play out. The guy in the launch stared at Richie. Richie stared at the guy in the launch. The other sailors in the other boats watched Richie and the guy in the launch. I didn't exist.

I'm getting the Harbor Patrol, the guy in the launch said.

I'll be here, Richie said.

The guy in the launch took off and the other boats went with him, though one or two hung back to watch Richie and me.

Are you going to right the fucker or not? Richie said; once again he towed me back out to the middle of the bay.

I was furious. I wanted Richie to listen to the guy in the launch. I wondered why Richie disliked me so to make me

97

suffer this way. I started swearing. Bellowing at the top of my lungs. Cussing out Richie without saying his name. And pulling. For all I was worth. The pontoon came out of the water a few times but went back down. This made me madder. I didn't care how much bigger Richie was than I, I was going to kick his ass when we got back on shore.

And then a strange thing happened. The pontoon came up and kept coming and the mast came out of the water and suddenly the boat was righted. The mast was in the air! All the lines dripped and water ran down the mast and I was on that trampoline so fast—but it was even colder out of the water than in because of the wind.

There, Richie said, you did it. And nobody helped.

My teeth chattered even more now and I could see that I was having deep shivers and I was still far too mad to say anything to Richie. But this feeling of accomplishment was beginning to overcome me.

Sail back and send out the next person, Richie said.

I just looked at him, still too grateful not to be in the drink with the mast underwater.

Go on, Richie said. Get in and get dressed.

When I hit shore some of the students looked at me with admiration while others commiserated with me about what an ass Richie was; he shouldn't have made a point with me.

I didn't help Richie store the boats that day. I didn't say anything to him. We crossed paths as the class was breaking up. He smiled at me. I just kept walking and didn't look back.

♦

Okay, if the preceding anecdote is allegorical, and it is, it's probably too Horatio Alger for you. It is for me, and the whole thing played out as I've retold it. I can see your point. Yet what's the alternative?

I drive a lot. I've checked out every title of Books on Tape that my library has. I've listened to all my music tapes until they're worn out. I've listened to baseball games and basketball games and football games. I've listened to the classical music station. The rap station. The oldies station. I've even listened to The Conservative, though only for a few days because The Conservative only has one idea—the excesses of Democratic bureaucrats. Like shooting fish in a barrel. (I'll be glad when the Roseanne/Rush Limbaugh era is over.)

This one day a talk show host, Larry Elder, who is libertarian, had on Don Jackson, the former Hawthorne police officer who captured on videotape a Long Beach police officer pushing him (Jackson) through a plate glass window. Some say Jackson provoked the incident by continuing to talk back to the police officer. And he did, but he was making a point. Blacks are treated differently by police. Don Jackson's point.

Larry Elder said, in essence, that Don Jackson was full of shit, the only way for blacks to make progress was for them to do it on their own, individually. Jackson said that Elder was full of shit, the only way for blacks to get their share was for them as a group to demand it from the government.

The "dialog" devolved into *ad hominem* attacks by both men. I've never desired to call a radio talk show. This one afternoon, however, I felt like talking to these two men.

Larry Elder said that the black middle-class professional didn't need any help. Don Jackson said that the black from South Central did need help. I wanted to tell these men that they were *both* right! Why are solutions all or nothing? Why can't there be disagreement without hatred? Maybe I was just listening to "good" radio, all the elements of drama, two diametrically opposed viewpoints whose proponents were battling it out verbally. Why are American issues of race only in black and white?

Affirmative Action was originally instituted to redress past injustices against blacks. Then the floodgates opened and every group that had been discriminated against climbed aboard because America doesn't have the best record vis-à-vis minority rights. Not the worst record either. Let's say there's room for improvement.

In my lifetime in Los Angeles, signs have been posted saying: no dogs or Mexicans. In my lifetime. In my lifetime Chicanos have been rounded up along with Mexican nationals and deported to Mexico. The United States is the birthplace for many people of Mexican descent, yet they've been routhinely deported to Mexico. U.S. citizens. Deported to another country, Mexico.

We know that segregation exists, think *barrio*. But segregation at one time was legally sanctioned, and not too long ago. There were "Mexican" sections or seats in movie theaters. There were "Mexican" days at public swimming pools. But even more sinister was the fact that schools were segregated. There were "Mexican" schools, even though the students were U.S. citizens. The U.S. Court of Appeals on April 14, 1947 upheld Mendez vs. four Orange County school districts (Westminster one of them, where I went to

Junior High School), effectively ending school-sanctioned segregation in California. This precedent was used in court during the civil rights movements in the 60s. Martin Luther King, Jr. is acknowledged as the father of contemporary American civil rights, and rightly so, but Gonzalo Mendez slew Goliath quietly and effectively almost two decades before King appeared on the national stage.

The population of Los Angeles is almost fifty percent Latino. There has never been a Latino mayor. There has never been a Chicano U.S. senator either. Or governor, since California joined the union. Go figure.

♦

What does all this have to do with Hobie Cats or Richie M? The sailing metaphor, of course. Nobody will help you when at sea.

That summer after my turtling experience Richie and I became friends. I'd go to his house on Friday or Saturday nights and we'd go out to eat. He let me come to the bay and take out a cat anytime I wished. He let me take any class I wanted that he taught, without registering or paying. We'd go to breakfast at Ma Barker's in Costa Mesa on our way down to the bay on early Saturday mornings.

Soon, I began teaching some of the beginning catamaran classes since I had a more recent knowledge of the dynamics associated with beginning sailing. I'd never sailed and had begun on cats. I could relate to what the students were feeling. They responded well to my guidance.

I also crewed for Richie's Offshore Sailing class. We'd take out a Westsail 46, a beamy, slow boat, but sturdy and we'd let the students do all the sailing. I and another guy, whose name I don't recall, would remain on deck and virtually run the class. Richie would go below and explain the rudiments of charts to students.

On days I wasn't with Richie I developed a ritual whereby I'd watch sunsets on the cliff overlooking Big Corona, the entrance to Newport Harbor. I wouldn't return home until all the lighted masts were safely within the confines of the breakwater. If something happened I could at least make a phone call, I reasoned. My justification. The reality was that I also liked my solitude those summer sunset nights in Corona del Mar. I'd see all kinds of couples and families going down to the fire rings at Big Corona, or lovers walking along the cliff, and local adolescents, carefree about time.

A few weekends a month I'd help Richie "sell" mini-catamarans at the Orange County Swapmeet. He'd bought out a business from a guy going belly-up, and had about ten of them assembled, with the molds and parts for another hundred. If they caught on, Richie reasoned, he'd make a bunch of money. They took up his entire backyard. We never sold any, although we drank beer and flirted a lot. And by then my nose was peeling and my hair, though black and thick, had that sun-crusted look of guys who spend their time on the water.

◆

Last night two girls came to the front door, selling candy. I didn't want any and told them so. My four-year old ran to the door to see what was going on. Followed by my wife.

They both wanted candy. So I called the girls back. I didn't want any candy since we were drinking wine and eating pizza, but my son wanted some for desert.

One of the girls was six-or seven-years old, the other possibly twelve. One had her hair in cornrows, the other had straightened her hair. They were both cute. Selling candy for the YMCA. The little girl made change from the backpack that the older girl wore. The little girl had to walk behind the other girl to do so.

While the transaction was going on my neighbor, a County Marshall, came over to ask the girls what they were selling. And how much. Friday afternoons at my neighbor's is a tradition around here. His friends from the marshal's office drink beer, talk shop and watch sports. All of them white men. Sometimes a lot of them. They are respectful, and when I first moved in, asked if they were too noisy, even though they had probably been meeting in that garage for well over fifteen years. They don't bother me in the least. Sometimes when our pizza is delivered they jokingly try to talk the delivery guy into selling *them* the pizza.

My neighbor only had one dollar, and in a spontaneous and kind gesture, he gave it to the girls. He didn't have enough for a box of candy, he said. All this sort of happened as a sidelight while the girls were making change for my wife. Except the little girl shorted my wife fifty cents. My wife asked for the correct change, which she got.

After the girls left and we got back to our wine and pizza, my wife said that she was embarrassed by our neighbor's behavior. He meant well, I said. It was a kind thing, I said. We all know what a decent man our neighbor is, my wife said. The girls weren't asking for money, they were selling candy, my wife said.

It was then that I wondered whether or not my neighbor would have done the same thing had the sellers of candy been white?

♦

There's a racial hierarchy in America, based not only race but also aligned economically and geographically. Areas that have huge numbers of browns, for example, are economically depressed, mostly in the American Southwest.

Britain is modeled after a class system. You are born into it. India is modeled after a caste system, something you are born into. Similarly, America is modeled after a racial system, something you are born into. I was born a Chicano, an American of Mexican descent (New Mexican, actually). Certain assumptions are made about me according to my height, my body type, my skin color, the color of my hair, where I grew up (Los Angeles), etc. When I was in elementary school a classmate told me I was from Texas. I'm from California, I told my classmate. No, you're not, he said. All Mexicans are from Texas, my classmate told me. I had to take that one home to my parents for an interpretation.

♦

Richie's words about nobody helping you at sea became prophetic, I learned, when I helped him deliver a new Westsail to San Francisco. The owner of the boat and his wife paid for the privilege of accompanying Richie and me on the shakedown cruise. The owner knew how to sail pretty well, better than I, but he didn't have the confidence to take his new boat out on the open sea.

Right off the bat, just on the fringe of Los Angeles Harbor, off San Pedro, we encountered a tug. No big deal. But she wasn't flying a flag alerting sailors that she was in tow, and had a cable that nobody saw. Richie, however, spotted the barge, but the cable was the deadly component. Richie noticed it in time, jibbed the boat, and averted an accident.

The owner and his wife and I were hot. We wanted to get on the ship-to-shore radio and call the harbor patrol, or the Coast Guard, someone to make that tug's captain accountable. Richie calmed us down, saying the close call was his fault. He should have been more aware, he said. Besides, he said, we'd be sailing in the shipping lanes off the California coast, and even if a freighter could slow or stop in time to avoid a collision, they wouldn't. This was a good wake up call, Richie said. So we sailed on.

It was just before Thanksgiving, the entire sky and ocean were one, drizzle alternating with clearing. Just off Point Conception the storm hit us. Gusts of wind to fifty knots. Rain and waves breaking over the boat. Everything in the boat wet. The owner and his wife didn't come on deck for twenty-four hours. I remained below for sixteen hours and only came up because Richie kicked my ass out. I'd been praying and shivering and puking, cowering in general, letting Richie reef the mainsail, letting him steer us on our course.

I told Richie that I wouldn't be able to keep my watch.

Richie said I could, I would, and there was no negotiating. He needed rest desperately, he said.

My head was spinning. I had puked everything out of my stomach, had the dry heaves, was cold and wet, and terrified. I'd never experienced anything remotely close to the power and naked energy unleashed on our tiny sailing vessel. Richie fell on the bunk I'd been in and was almost asleep.

I remembered the turtled catamaran.

What do I do? I said.

Look for ships, Richie said. When we're on the tops of waves, look for lights. You won't see anything when we're in the troughs.

What about our course?

We're on auto pilot. Keep us on the current heading, unless we're in the path of a ship. Wake me if you see a ship.

And he was out.

I went above into the raging sea. The mainsail was fully reefed and we were heading into the wind, which also happened to be the direction we wanted to go, but we made little progress. I wrapped a line around my arm, huddled in the cockpit behind the wheel, and tried to remain awake, to keep my watch, and I did. What I remember is this: I didn't care whether I lived or died, I was that frightened. My stomach was trying to escape out my esophagus, release itself into the air. I wanted to stop moving. I wished I could see. I wanted there not to be water everywhere. I wanted to be dry. I wanted everything to be over, stop this tremendous struggle. I stood my watch.

By the next afternoon the wind began to subside. The third day we hit some blue sky. Red sky at night, sailor's delight. And it's true. The owner's wife made a celebratory dinner, complete with wine, but I didn't feel like celebrating my lack of spirit, my fear, and besides, I thought I'd never drink alcohol again in this lifetime. Nobody mentioned the storm, or our behavior. It was just something we'd encountered and left behind.

I learned some things about myself that night on deck with the wind raging all about me and the sea breaking over the bow of the boat. I learned I wasn't a sailor. I was too relieved to be sailing under the Golden Gate, too happy to see cars, to get my ass in sheltered waters. Land and cars and that bridge were the promised land. I wasn't a sailor. Not the kind that can circumnavigate the globe single-handed. I didn't have that driving desire to conquer the sea. The ocean had squashed my spirit like a roach, no doubt about it. I wasn't a sailor.

Richie and I stayed at the Oakland Yacht Club that night. After having dinner with the owner and his wife at a restaurant that supposedly had been frequented by Jack London. Richie knew a woman who had a big trimaran docked in the harbor. I slept on the trampoline in a sleeping bag, Richie slept belowdecks with the woman. She took us to the airport the next day.

We were flush with money from the sail, and I don't remember where we got the cocaine, but I remember snorting some in the bathroom before boarding our plane. Sort of a celebration, I suppose. And I remember drinking beer on the flight, and laughing about the storm.

◆

I moved to Newport Beach after the breakup with my

girlfriend. We had lived together more than two years, and for all purposes were married—at least I considered myself married. We'd met in college, as I've said. In the Northwest. She was from Oregon, and came from money. I was from California. My parents had no money to speak of.

And this: She was married when we fell in love. I helped to destroy a marriage. When we began living together, while still in the Northwest, she heard a lot of stuff about how she'd left her husband for a Mexican.

Her father was of Swedish descent. More than once he said to me, Wouldn't you be more comfortable with one of your own kind? When we broke up for good, her father told me I might be able to meet one of my own kind at a Catholic church.

I remember all this because when I had met Richie I was particularly down. Not only heartsick at having lost an important relationship, I also had the additional grief of the racial comments her father had heaped on me. I wore those hurtful remarks like a yoke, like a beast of burden plowing a minefield. I didn't feel very good about myself in those days.

It was Richie who helped me begin my ascent when out of the blue he told me I was good. I won't digress into any psychobabble about self-esteem, other than to say somebody made me feel good about myself. And it was Richie. And I can't forget this.

In those days in Orange County there weren't many minorities living along the coast. And I doubt there are even now. The mayor of Newport Beach, the saying goes, said that Mexicans could mow lawns in the daytime, but he wanted them out of town by sunset. Another rumor circulated which stated the code word the police dispatchers used when a black person was in Newport was NIN. Nigger in Newport.

The reason this rumor was in circulation was that a black man had been shot by police in front of the Albertson's, where I did my shopping. In Corona del Mar. Which is part of Newport Beach, even though we had our own post office. The town was patrolled by Newport Beach police officers. It seemed the Bank of America had been robbed, by black men, and the fellow who was shot had made the error of leaving Albertson's at the same time the police were pursuing bank robbers. The man shot wasn't involved in the robbery. Most people I spoke with about the incident were pleased with the performance by the police. The younger people I knew were mostly appalled by the event. They weren't yet voting age, but had they been, they probably wouldn't have voted anyway.

◆

After our return from San Francisco Richie and I became closer than ever. I was taken to his mother's house for a barbecue, and here I met Julie, a woman I'd seen a number of times at Richie's house, but now knew that they were very connected, for she was treated as part of the family. Julie was blonde, not very tall, but strong, and drove a Jeep a decade before it became fashionable. The term soulmates comes to mind when I think of Richie and Julie, sort of like George Burns and Gracie Allen, or my mother and father. It was as if Julie knew about all of Richie's carousing, but let him have it for she knew they'd be together later. And I'm sure they would have married, had Richie lived long enough.

The contractor I worked for was going to have a two-month hiatus in work. We were busy, trying to finish our jobs before the layoff period. We'd been working without pause more than two years, and I was looking forward to the break. The guys with families got on elsewhere, temporarily.

I was single, had a bunch of money saved, and wanted to do something decisive. There was a Kittridge 36 woodhull for sale, with a mooring right behind The Crab Cooker in Newport Harbor. I had enough for a large down payment, then I could live aboard. But I remembered my behavior during the storm. Maybe I could discipline myself not to run in the face of danger at sea, but I knew that, left to my own devices on that trip, I would have huddled below willing to let whatever was going to happen, happen. Not the best strategy for sailing. Or for anything.

My girlfriend and I had been planning on traveling in Europe before some health problems arose for her. We didn't go, yet a trip to Europe was still on my mind. I thought that my undergraduate education was not complete until I'd seen much of the art in Europe. And I was right, as it turned out.

Also, Richie had a delivery to Seattle, and asked that I crew for him. Around this time we had undergone a slow withdrawal from one another. He was snorting a lot of coke. And he'd given up some of the sailing classes to rig a boat for some rich guy. The rich guy had started a bank account in Richie's name so that Richie wouldn't have to waste time asking for money. He could rig the boat to his desires, no questions asked. Except Richie was spending a lot of money on cocaine and chintzing on the outfitting costs. The rich guy didn't know the difference. Once, a woman I knew from one of Richie's classes and whom I dated called me one afternoon to say that Richie had begun a class and disappeared. Then I heard that the city was going to fire him.

All things considered, I went to Europe instead of buying the Kittridge, instead of sailing upwind with Richie to Seattle. And I don't regret that decision.

After my return from Europe I went to Richie's house. As soon as I arrived I knew he no longer lived there. No catamarans in the backyard. No sails strewn about the front yard. No cars parked on the lawn. No dogs.

Work was really cookin' and my employers were glad to have me back—I'd taken an extra month. I settled into a work routine for the rest of winter. It had been over a year since the San Francisco sail.

One night my younger brother and I went to the movies at the Balboa Theater. A Fellini film, I think. After the show we went to The Studio Café for a drink. While at the bar with my brother I saw Julie, Richie's girlfriend, the one he always ended up with, the one he'd known forever, the one who knew his mother, as I did. Julie was with a friend who was pretty far gone. I could tell as we exchanged introductions. I told Julie where I'd been all this time. Then I said that I'd been to Richie's but it appeared he'd moved.

All Julie said was: You don't know, do you?

I said, Know what?

Neither woman responded. My brother was watching the jazz trio.

Tell me, I said.

Julie's friend swiveled on her bar stool and said, Richie went to the big sailboat in the sky. Then she giggled. At her witty euphemism, I supposed.

Julie looked into my soul and gave me sympathy and empathy and caring.

I ordered two double scotches. Then I asked my brother to take me home.

Julie told me to get in touch with her and she'd tell me about it. We made a date for Friday night.

When I went to her house this is what she told me: Richie began doing more and more drugs. His last day he did a quarter ounce of cocaine. He had a seizure while in bed and Julie called 911. With his last bit of strength, Richie had thrown off the paramedics who were trying to help him. After that they just watched Richie die. Overdose. OD'd.

I looked at Julie. She hugged me as we sat on her little couch.

You can cry, Julie said, a lot of people did.

◆

If we subscribe to existing racial stereotypes, the tall white "hunk" isn't supposed to die of a cocaine overdose. We'd buy that the Mexican could. The tall gorgeous white guy who is desired by Hollywood, the guy who has his picture on the cover of *Sail Magazine*, sheeting in the mainsail in a fierce wind with the twelve meter heeled over about thirty degrees, and every other guy in the photo is simply hanging on, well, this guy isn't supposed to OD. Maybe the shorter Mexican would. You'd expect that, you'd certainly not think twice about it if you were to see it in a film, for example.

A few years ago a black activist group chided Jews in

Hollywood for not portraying blacks in a better light in films. I read about it in the *Metro* section of the *Los Angeles Times.* The column next to it was about a flower grower in Oxnard who was being brought up on federal slavery charges for incarcerating Mexican immigrants against their wills in an escape-proof compound—barbed wire, high fences, etc. They owed their souls to the company store. All this was laid out in an article in which their lawyer was interviewed. The plaintiffs didn't speak English. The lawyer was representing them *pro bono,* and had a distinctly Jewish sounding last name. (You know the stereotype, the bulldog Jewish lawyer).

After World War II my parents built their first home. My father had served in the Navy, twenty-seven months straight in the Pacific arena, while my mother had lived with his parents on Brooklyn Avenue in East Los Angeles, worked and saved her money, also saved every check my father sent her so that they had enough for a down payment.

Many places they looked for their first home they were told that Mexicans weren't desirable in the area. My parents grew up in Boyle Heights in East Los Angeles. Both of their families were originally from New Mexico. But still, they'd lived in California long enough to know that this was how things were. But my father had just returned from a war and he couldn't help but be stung by the overt racism directed toward him and his family. At that time in Los Angeles Jews weren't allowed to join many country clubs and blacks went to a segregated beach.

My parents bought a lot in Lynwood and had a custom home built, since they weren't wanted in the new housing tracts. While the house was under construction one of the neighbors circulated a petition to try to stop Mexicans from moving into the neighborhood. The story goes that a Jewish neighbor squelched the petition by pointing out the fact to other neighbors that we'd just fought a war over this kind of thinking.

◆

I've bought a house during a recession that's gripped California like a small python the last eight years. If it hadn't been for falling real estate prices my wife and I would have probably never been able to afford a house in California. And this too: We bought in the Inland Empire. An area that includes San Bernardino, Riverside and Redlands, where we live, among other cities. As the name implies, it's inland. Away from the beach.

When I was in my twenties, after my time with Richie, I was self-employed, my crew remodeling a shopping center. In Fontana. Also in the Inland Empire. Every day when working it would be ninety-five to one-hundred-and-five degrees. On the drive back to Corona del Mar, we would be shirtless, the hot desert wind blowing around the truck's cab. Around Anaheim Hills, we would put on T-shirts. Somewhere on the Newport Freeway we'd put on our sweatshirts. By the time we got home, to Corona del Mar, right on the beach, the windows would be up. Had we been in Corona del Mar all day, it would have been another typically pleasant and mild day. But when the temperature drops over thirty degrees in less than an hour—as it did on the commute from Fontana to Corona del Mar—it really affects your body. I mention all this to illustrate the difference in climate between the desirable temperate ocean air and the less forgiving desert air, where the smog level is "unhealthful" every day of the summer, where I must live because of affordability.

I have a phobia about the heat. At the beginning of July, as it is now, I'm looking at at least one hundred days of temperatures above ninety-five degrees. Hotter when there's a "heat wave." Both of my paternal grandparents suffered strokes during heat waves in Los Angeles. My father is a stroke victim as well, though his was not hastened by the heat. Still, I'm afraid of the heat and I'm afraid of stroke. I stay in the house a good part of the "summer."

Obviously the climate in the Inland Empire is not as desirable as the one encountered next to the ocean. But it's cheaper here. We can afford a house. And there's a healthy mix of races here as well: blacks, browns, whites.

When I lived along the coast in Orange County the only "Mexicans" you saw were those mowing lawns. The only blacks, years ago, lived in Santa Ana. Now Santa Ana is almost exclusively Latino. There weren't many minorities in Orange County in those days. The Inland Empire, however hot, has a diverse population. When I go shopping I see brown people and black people and white people, which makes me more comfortable than simply seeing one racial group. When I shopped in Corona del Mar there wasn't a mix of people, there was only one group, and I was secretly apprehensive as a result.

The house I bought has not appreciated in the last two years. In fact, it's worth less than when we bought, and we purchased at the bottom of the real estate fall. One of the reasons for the lack of appreciation for my house is that demographics are changing. I feel quite enlightened when I see students walking in groups that contain whites and browns and blacks. I'm not the least bit apprehensive when I see an entire group of brown children walking together. However, when I see a group composed entirely of black children, something happens, and I don't like this. I don't like my apprehension. I want there to be white or brown children with them. Why is this? What is this? The awareness of the racial hierarchy, is what it is.

Have I had bad experiences with black children? No. With black adults? No. When I was a child growing up in Los Angeles there was a huge influx of black people into our neighborhood. I saw a news clip on television the other day. It showed my old school, Woodcrest Elementary School, where parents were escorting their children to school. Every parent interviewed was black. There was a molester, a black man, preying on children. All the parents and children shown in the news clip were black.

When I lived in that neighborhood about five-ten percent of the population was black. There has been a change in demographics, one could say. Shortly after we moved, the Watts riots flared. I was glad we no longer lived there.

Once when I was walking to Woodcrest Elementary School in the morning, a group of high school boys, all black, got me in a circle and pushed me around. They didn't hurt me, and I don't think it even bothered me that much at the time—boys did that sort of thing to other boys, where I grew up.

Another time, on a Saturday afternoon, my father sent me to the big Winchell's Donuts on Normandie and Century to get some donuts. A spontaneous treat for our working-class family. I rode my bike. On the ride home a pickup truck cut me off right on Normandie. The bed of the truck was filled with boys, some of them my age, some of them younger. There were three men in the cab of the pickup. One of the men got out of the cab, walked over to me, and asked directions. I turned to point the way for him, and he snatched the box of donuts out of my grasp. The boys in the bed of the truck couldn't have known what this ignorant ass was going to do, but after he did it, they all began laughing. They were black.

I flushed with rage. I cried with rage. The truck drove off with my donuts, the boys still laughing at me. I returned home empty-handed, and my father drove around the neighborhood streets, looking for those men. We didn't find them, and I was secretly glad we didn't.

When in graduate school and I began student teaching, a number of my students in the composition classes were black. They were good students, but they spoke Black Standard English, a dialect. If they wrote their papers in their own "voices," they received lower grades because Black Standard English allows double negatives, among other nonconforming aspects of Standard English, and I was compelled to enforce Standard English in those days as a teaching assistant. Once when talking with my students during office hours I asked them where they were from. Los Angeles, one said. Where? I said. Crenshaw, another said. Do you know Sportsman's Park? I said. They knew it well, though they told me it was named Jesse Owens Park, and they probably had the same fond memories of long summer afternoons at the pool. The park became a bond

117

between us. It felt good.

A few months before the Rodney King beating was captured on videotape for the entire planet to see, one of my
students was relating in a class how he'd been arrested
over the weekend in Newport Beach. He was a good student. But he was stopped for no reason, he said. When he
demanded to know why he was being stopped, he was
beaten and arrested for resisting arrest. I remembered NIN.
Many of the students in my class discounted his story. Then
the Rodney King thing happened. My student's story now
had credibility for the other students. The student I speak
of was black. He was beaten for questioning, something he
was taught to do in college.

Does your racial makeup matter in an emergency? In
sailing, no. During a race riot in Los Angeles, yes.

What do we do?

Acknowledge the hierarchy. And move on. Americans
are race aware, no question about it. Racial awareness may
be directly proportional to the darkness of your skin. How
much melanin you're born with. America is not color blind.

A color-blind nation is desirable, noble even, and is
something to aspire toward. We're not there yet, however.
Not even close. The Horatio Alger metaphor works for
some while it doesn't work for others. Some people "make
it" entirely on their own. Ward Connerly has. Made it on
his own. Except he's got state contracts for his business.
And his friend is the governor, which doesn't hurt, one
assumes. Others are unable to make it on their own. I'm
one of the latter. I've been helped by the government. But
then everyone in the U.S. has been helped by the government, whether it's in the form of tax breaks, or welfare, or

using roads, we've all been helped by the government. In one way or another.

🌑 Acknowledge the hierarchy. It exists. If you're Native American certain assumptions will be made about you. The same if you're English or French or German or Angolan or Cuban or Mexican or Israeli or Egyptian. Certain assumptions will be made about you, depending upon where your ancestors hale from. This is not necessarily a bad thing. It's more a starting point. Until you know the individual. You can never know the group. You can know individuals. Acknowledge and move on.

There are a few people for whom the hierarchy doesn't exist. Richie M was one of these people. Years later after my time with Richie I worked for a man called Mr. Paul. Mr. Paul was a Polish Jew who got off the boat in New York in winter and sold his coat for ten dollars so that he could eat, the story goes. In the late seventies, when I worked for Mr. Paul, who was quite old by this time, he donated one million dollars to the City of Hope. In those days a million dollars was really something. In those days a professional athlete who was making fifty thousand dollars was adequately compensated. The racial hierarchy did not exist for Mr. Paul. He judged you on the quality of your work. And a high school friend comes to mind. Brad P. I can't recall race being an issue for him. I have no idea how many people I've encountered in my lifetime thus far. Yet only three people were unaware of the hierarchy, in my memory at least. Maybe this is convenient, selective recall to propel my thesis. I'm sure there were others, weren't there?

THE RELENTLESS PURSUIT OF
THE UNITED STATES CALVARY

I'VE BEEN ON SABBATICAL. Sabbatical comes from the Hebrew word sabbath, or day of rest. The seventh day is one of rest. Sabbatical year meant that every seven years certain fields would lie fallow so the land could rejuvenate. In a sabbatical year in biblical terms the slaves were released as well. Sabbatical now only applies to academics, I believe. And where I teach you get a sabbatical semester, not a year. If you can afford it, you can take off the entire school year at one-half pay .

As the term originally implied, sabbatical is a time of rest or rejuvenation. Except where I teach, the system has no money, and it's also beholdin' to the political whims of those in Sacramento, the state's capital. If one is junior faculty where I teach, one must write a superb grant proposal in order to secure a sabbatical leave. If one is senior faculty, one must wait anywhere from nine to nineteen years to get a sabbatical leave.

For those who work full-time jobs and who get two weeks off, if they're lucky, the concept of sabbatical leave may seem ludicrous. But keep in mind that academics are not compensated to the same extent of those in business.

Academics have job security, get great periods of time off to pursue their own work, but are paid only a fraction of what one may earn in business. Ergo, don't compare the compensation of an academic with that of a salesman, for example; you'd be comparing orchids and cacti.

During my eight months off—the regular semester and summer break—I've written almost two hundred pages of essays. Seventy-five pages of a new novel. And done extensive research. If given the time, I could be a real writer, a full-time writer. Not that I could make money at it, however.

I was on campus yesterday to make copies of the work I'm presently involved in. I crossed paths with an unpleasant liberal dinosaur, a man who's now retired. One of the ones who feels he is responsible for establishing Pan African Studies, Chicano Studies, etc. And he did help in those areas, I'm sure. Except for him time has stood still, forever frozen in the sixties, his heyday, his glory years, when he marched for students' rights.

The unpleasant dinosaur—he's huge, coincidentally, taking us back to the time when the largest ruled—told me he's seen my name here and there. Then he said, I wonder why he's in there? he doesn't even speak Spanish. Yes, he spoke to me in the third person.

♦

When the unpleasant dinosaur said why is he in there? he was making reference to all the anthologies and journals my fiction and essays have been in. I've been lucky; I've been included in much of the "Latino boom" in American letters. No books, though. Many short pieces.

♦

Upon my hiring at CSU, Northridge, the English Department arranged a luncheon with some members of the Chicano Studies Department. Ostensibly to get their approval for my hiring. To see if I could eat with a knife and fork, one of the people attending told me in private. The English Department search committee didn't know whether or not I was "Chicano" enough for their colleagues in Chicano Studies, ergo the luncheon with the School of Humanities Dean, the Vice President for Academic Affairs, and the Chicano Studies faculty members. When I interviewed with the English Department search and screen committee, I was asked if I spoke Spanish. I was interviewing for a job as professor of English, teaching fiction writing. I was an Affirmative Action hire. I had obtained my Master of Fine Arts degree from a major university writing program. Prior to my hiring at Northridge, I was not even given an interview at those places where I'd applied. I was asked to apply to Northridge by the chair of the search and screen committee. I didn't even know they were hiring, and had I known, I wouldn't have applied—the school is ninety miles from where I live. But there it is. I was solicited for the job. I was hired. I was an Affirmative Action hire.

When I attended the luncheon with my future colleagues nothing was mentioned about the circumstances of my hiring, though I figured they knew I was entering the job under the auspices of Affirmative Action

♦

The unpleasant dinosaur told me fondly of the "Chicago Mafia," my first week on the job. At the copy machine, where all the action occurs. This is what the Chicago Mafia consisted of: All faculty members hired for a time had their degrees from the University of Chicago. He didn't say that they were all white and male. And large. Like pro linemen.

◆

My first weeks on the job I was paired with a "mentor," a senior faculty member who might show me the ropes at the institution. When I was hired there were almost thirty thousand students. After tuition hikes and the Northridge Earthquake, enrollments dropped. Now there are just over twenty-seven thousand students. My mentor took me out to dinner as part of his duties. All you'll get here is one free meal, my mentor told me. He gave it to me. The unpleasant dinosaur and the really unpleasant dinosaur were friends with my mentor. They came along for the dinner, probably my second or third week on the job.

The really unpleasant dinosaur told me that the department had wanted to hire a guy from Texas. A guy with a Ph.D., to teach writing, fiction, to undergraduates and graduates. Ph.D.s, in my opinion, shouldn't teach fiction, because, as the student said, Those guys only use half their brains, and it's the wrong half. But that's another story.

◆

How the unpleasant dinosaur got his name: During my first semester, I was returning from the library with a bunch of books. I was researching the collective unconscious and Jung and magic realism. I waited for the elevator at the Tower, where the faculty offices for my department are located. The unpleasant dinosaur arrived, and waited with me. Another faculty member arrived, one who was from India, it was evident, by his speech. The unpleasant dinosaur asked the professor from India what caste was he? Then to me he said, after looking at my books, You either know it by now or you don't.

◆

How the really unpleasant dinosaur got his name: I'm at the copy machine, where you're fair game. The really unpleasant dinosaur was all worked up because Blank hadn't gotten release time. In those days there were two competitions for grants—Scholarly Research and Creative Activity, or Affirmative Action. Blank couldn't apply for an Affirmative Action grant because he was a white male. This infuriated the really unpleasant dinosaur. The really unpleasant dinosaur said to me, What's Blank supposed to do? He 'ain't got a cunt and his name ain't López. I was new on the job. I was seeing red. My options were to bash him right there on the spot, or to walk away. I don't believe in violence; however, I still wish I'd had the *juevos* to let him have it right there in the English Department mail room. I walked out without responding to him. My father always told me to fight only when attacked.

◆

We finished our dinner, my mentor, me, the unpleasant dinosaur and the really unpleasant dinosaur, with the really unpleasant dinosaur telling me that I was free. They had really wanted the other guy, the guy from Texas, but the vice president had thrown me in at no cost to the Department. How you going to turn that down? the really unpleasant dinosaur said.

◆

When Blank came up for promotion and tenure—we were hired the same year, but I received early promotion and tenure because of my many publications—I was on the personnel committee reviewing Blank's file. In five years at the school, Blank had not one publication. He claimed he had written an article which he was sending out. The senior faculty members on the committee all beamed their approval at Blank. The other junior faculty member on the committee besides myself asked Blank, Where is the essay? The alleged essay wasn't in his file with all his other materials. Blank said he'd get it to us. I don't recall ever seeing it.

◆

The canon must be preserved. If you let those people into the exhibit, into the magazine, into the neighborhood, into the college, you'll be lowering standards.

◆

The assumption was that Henry Cisneros would have to brush up on his Spanish if he wanted to pursue higher public office. This was, of course, before the scandal broke over his extra-marital affair. Then it got worse. He paid off his paramour. Or stopped paying her. Or something. And she sued him. Henry Cisneros had to settle for an appointed position. A cabinet position. I don't know whether or not he brushed up on his Spanish.

♦

Do you live here? the little girl asked. She was on a swing. In the backyard behind my parents' house. At the high part of each swingpush her head was above the back fence.

Yes, my father answered. He was putzing in the backyard, pruning and planting flowers, doing the things that retirees do in the backyard in the sun in the springtime.

Do you live with a woman? the little girl asked.

I live with my wife, my father said.

The little girl's head went back and forth, back and forth, up and down, up and down. Above the wall, behind the wall. Is she brown too? the little girl asked.

What difference does it make? my father said.

Later, when relating the story to me, my father said, You get that shit in your own yard.

He had been working in the sun. His parents, my grandparents, were dark. His hair was white. He was *brown*, my father.

♦

N. Scott Momaday, the Pulitzer Prize winning poet and oral storyteller, said his Kiowa ancestors were unable to withstand the relentless pursuit of the U.S. Calvary. None of the aboriginal North American people were able to withstand this onslaught.

♦

You're new on the block, renting. Yet already you tell people where to park, not in front of your house, and it's a city street. Your husband stops at the house two, three, four times a day in his city police cruiser. You guys mow your lawn religiously every Friday afternoon whether or not it needs mowing. You have 2.5 children, the .5 in your belly.

♦

If you have a million dollars you can emigrate to the U.S. No questions asked.

♦

Spike Lee's worst film made all the "best" lists because the film was about a white guy's pizzeria getting torched by black guys.

♦

Your first month on the block you hacked the juniper bushes on either side of the front door with kitchen knives, scissors, wire cutters, anything you could get your hands on, and in the afternoon, by golly, those bushes were down.

♦

Paul Robeson split.

♦

Does Ross Perot speak French? Will he have to brush up on it to run for office again?

♦

Did John Kennedy speak Gaelic? Did he have to learn it to become president?

♦

Did Martin Luther King speak Ibo? Was he supposed to learn it? Was he expected to give speeches in Ibo?

♦

This is what I'm saying: If you're Latino you're held to a different standard. Not only am I expected to know American and British Literature, but I'm also supposed to be an expert on anything written in Spanish. I'm supposed to know and like every minority writer. The truth of the matter is I'm not familiar with everything written in Spanish— no one person is. The truth of the matter is, I like some minority writers and not others. I go where my interests lie. I go to the library. I read all the time, unlike the unpleasant dinosaur, evidently.

♦

Publication is a criterion for promotion, where I teach. There are three categories: Professional Achievements (publication fits into this category); Teaching; and Service (to the department, to the school, to the university, and to the community).

After four years at the university I went up for promotion. Technically it was early, the manual dictates a normal cycle as six years. Except that everyone was getting tenure and promoted in four years. So I went up. I had excellent teaching evaluations. I had numerous publications in major anthologies. I had served on department committees, school committees, university committees, and had done a number of readings at bookstores and universities in the community.

My department personnel committee recommended that I be given tenure and promoted. My department chair recommended that I be given tenure and promoted. The school personnel committee recommended that I be given tenure and promoted. The school dean recommended that I be given tenure and promoted. In short, I was given unanimous approval for tenure and promotion by all those associated with the promotion process. Many of my colleagues congratulated me on my promotion and tenure. There was still one more committee left to review my file, but it was pro forma, since that committee existed to help candidates appeal negative recommendations. Everyone said it was a done deal, my promotion and tenure.

The year I went up for tenure and promotion, we also had a new president of the university. Sometime before my file left the review committee, the new president visited them, telling them they were no longer a rubber stamp committee. They would now review all files. In the past, when the candidate was unanimously approved, the review committee didn't bother with those files—they simply followed the recommendations of the earlier committees. The new president changed horses in the middle of the race, as the saying goes.

To make a long story short, the review committee, in place to help candidates appeal *unfavorable* recommendations, overturned my unanimous recommendations. The committee told me I was making good progress toward eventual tenure and promotion. The earlier committees didn't say I was making progress, however, they said I had earned the promotion and tenure now. Yet the review committee decided to "kick back" the files of two Latinos and another male. This was the spring Chicano students were fasting at UCLA to gain departmental status for Chicano Studies.

My colleague, who's adept at legalese, drafted a letter saying we would sue the president and the committee members, if they didn't reconsider their vote. To make another long story short, the way the committee was caught with its pants down was the fact that since we, my colleague and I, were such strong candidates, we were not allowed to participate in the appeal process, the reason for the existence of the review committee in the first place. Had we not received unanimous recommendations, then we would have been entitled to an appeal/appearance before the review committee. I was subsequently given tenure and promotion.

♦

When Blank came up for promotion and tenure, six years into it, during the normal cycle, rather than early, he had no publications, as I've stated. He had weak teaching evaluations. He had nominal service. He had what is called a "thin" file—nothing in it, literally. However, he was recommended by all the committees for promotion and tenure. The school dean, however, didn't recommend him for tenure or promotion. The dean's negative recommendation was overturned by the review committee. The same committee that overturned my unanimous recommendation. I liked Blank okay. He was nothing to me. Just your typical mediocre coworker. When he was hired, the existing rules were such that he expected to get promoted and to get tenure. It wasn't his fault they changed horses in the race.

♦

I don't have a problem with Blank getting tenure and promoted. I do have a problem with the way the review committee handled my case. It's a committee comprised of senior faculty members. The faculty senate president, who is automatically on the committee, broke ranks and wrote a letter asking the committee to reconsider my file. And the file of my colleague. The President ordered the committee to grant my colleague and me an interview. Senior faculty.

Union members.

Who acted in this fashion.

One theory was that the committee was playing chicken with the new president, using my colleague and me as bait. That was one theory.

I don't know why this happened to me. I don't much care anymore. It did create a level of cynicism in me vis-à-vis the academic environment that I formerly didn't have. I know I was not the only one to be subjected to this form of hazing. It goes with the territory, I suppose.

◆

My father always taught me to be an individual, to shun the "group," when possible. I was taught that by being better individually, I would be able to better the group. So I was trained to better myself. It also happened that at this time I was co-chair of La Raza Faculty and Staff Association. Other than playing team sports, I've only been involved in clubs or organizations a few times in my life.

In high school in the eleventh grade I was in a club called Beta Sig. When a senior in high school I belonged to the Sunset Beach Surf Club. Now, I'm in the Chicano Surfing Association, a club I started with a novelist friend. The Chicano Surfing Association is a response to our mutual frustration with the world of publishing. In those days I belonged to La Raza Faculty and Staff Association.

I was ambivalent about my involvement in a group that was based solely upon race. I'm not sure that I will necessarily have anything in common with a person, based solely upon our race. Still, I wished to support Latinos in the university, thus my involvement. And the notion that we might derive power from our group. And we did, for the chink in the armor of the review committee, I later found out, was a direct result of the intervention of the former faculty senate president, a member of La Raza Faculty and Staff Association, on my behalf, to the current faculty senate president. When I was singled out by the powerful review committee, all the other recommending committees came to my aid. In the normal channels. But the letter from the former faculty senate president got further results. I'm still ambivalent about the Association, yet I'm aware enough to know that my membership in it did help me, however roundabout.

The thing is, the meetings of the powerful committees are confidential.

That's how everyone gets away with their dirty work. The really devious moves are done by committee, in secret, under the cloak of confidentiality.

I was a far better candidate than Blank. The committee furthest removed from me, and the one that was in place to look out for my rights, trampled upon them. In Blank's case, the committee functioned in its normal capacity—they gave him a hearing and felt compelled to overturn a negative recommendation.

♦

If one were to get one's sense of the American West from old John Ford movies, one might think that the Irish played a pivotal role in the settlement of the West. This may be so, though it may be inaccurate just as easily. I don't know.

John Ford wasn't making documentaries, he was making films. Hollywood isn't responsible for verisimilitude, for portraying historical events accurately—think Demi Moore as Hester Prynne (I didn't see the film, she may have been good in the role). I like old John Ford movies, even though I've cringed, physically squirmed, when they show the subservient "Mexican" servants. Still, I like his films, and I even like the Duke. A lot.

I don't mean to put down John Ford or Irish people. On the contrary, I have a spiritual affinity with things Irish, something that may be akin to their yearning for the past. Something that is fiercely as proud of my past as Ford seemed to be of his.

◆

It's just that there's yet to be a filmmaker exaggerating and embellishing *my* past, celebrating *my* past, on the big screen.

◆

In spite of the fact that this is a semi-arid climate, you've recreated a Midwest habitat, right here in the desert. You have a two-story house complete with a picket fence surrounded by deciduous trees, and a green, green lawn, even in a drought, especially in a drought. You create lakes, and cement the arroyos, and then make fun of them because they are cemented. You make fun of the geography because there's no water. Sort of like making fun of Manhattan because it's surrounded by water. If the land weren't

134

"transformed" into the magical re-creation of the Midwest, there'd be only chaparral and cacti. Palm Springs now has humidity problems because of all the swimming pools and green lawns. Green lawns in the middle of the desert!

◆

After the trial of the century, Robert Shapiro to Johnnie Cochran, Why did you play the race card?

Johnnie Cochran to Robert Shapiro, Everything's about race.

◆

When I was a faculty senator, an elected position, I heard another senator give an impassioned speech as to why we should not consider race as a criterion for admission or employment at our university. This was the same man who wouldn't look at me when I had my interview with the review committee that discriminated against me. A man arguing for a color-blind society. When he was part of the gang that singled me out because of my race. I don't know what Martin Luther King would say to my colleague, or to Ward Connerly. Would he embrace them? Shun them? I don't know.

◆

The outspoken critic of Affirmative Action, the regent appointed by his close personal friend, the Governor, is either disingenuous or stupid if he thinks he has no effect

on the admissions officer to whom he is personally handing a student's file for further review after that student has
been turned down by UC. This is affirmative action. This is
what has always been in place. "Who you know," it's
called. How many other minority regents sit on the board?
How many minority candidates will have their files
reviewed if this is the only affirmative action in place?

♦

When I was finally "allowed" an interview in front of the
review committee, the committee that was supposed to
look out for my rights, I had to commute to school on a day
that I wasn't scheduled to teach. For most people this
would not be a big deal. People who work five days a week
would say, Quit whining, everyone goes in everyday, and
they're right, except hourly people do not bring work
home (at least they didn't used to). And this: it's ninety
miles one way to my place of employ. That's my personal
cross to bear, but there it is, I had to commute on a day that
I normally wouldn't have. With the prospect of tenure and
more money—I must say here that after my first year, my
salary was frozen, with no debate—my wife and I were
considering buying a home instead of renting. All bets
were off now, however. I was in a dark mood.

I shaved and showered and was getting dressed in my
study, the room set aside for my writing, where I kept all
my clothes since my wife's took up all the other available
closet space in the house. As I said, I was in a dark mood. I
was angry. Angry "they" had done this to me; angry I had
to go in an extra day; angry I had to appear before a bunch

of asinine bureaucrats. It was spring, which is already quite warm in Redlands. I was hot, in a dark humor. When I tried to close my closet door after getting my clothes out, it became stuck. I pushed on it. The door suddenly became metaphor—my poor state, a cheap rental house where things didn't work, and I was getting my nose rubbed in my race. I pushed the door again. It was a big old heavy wooden one. It wouldn't budge. I let all my fury loose on that door, and boy, did it move!

The further problem was that my toddler was now at my leg, unknown to me, peering into the closet, in the path of the heavy door. The door hit my son in the head, and made a hollow clunk like a bowling ball hitting the hardwood floor. He screamed. I picked him up. My wife flew into the room. Snatched my son from me.

I'm not quite sure of the sequence after that. I next found myself in the hallway, with my knees lowered, square to the wall (lath and plaster here, no sissy drywall for me), where I proceeded to *oi-zuki* the wall. A front punch to the mid-section. The hand stopped on the hard surface, energy vibrating along the knuckles until it hit the weakest link, the bone behind the little finger, a boxer's break it's called, and there I stood, with my son wailing in the background, and the bone in my right hand shifted back a few centimeters.

I got really hot and light headed. My wife and son were next to me. Then I was on the couch. My son was rubbing my head. They gave me a Coke. They gave me a washcloth with ice in it. My hand was huge. After a time on the couch I got up, finished dressing, then drove the ninety miles for my "meeting."

Part of the problem was: There were twenty-one candidates

unanimously recommended for early promotion and tenure. The review committee, in place to help candidates appeal negative recommendations, singled out two Latinos. This is the opposite of affirmative action. It's action, of that there can be no doubt, and it's negative action, the opposite of affirmative action. And it happens all the time. In the academic world, *de rigueur.*

The day after my appearance before the review committee, I went to the doctor. After the x-rays, he "mashed" my hand back into place. Then my hand was encased in plaster.

♦

While eight months pregnant you painted the entire house, with a four-inch brush, and man, you're won over, you've got to admire that spirit. That tenacity. Though you don't have a clue as to its origin. You're in the dark as to where the stuff comes from. The sheer stubborn will of Arthur to extract Excaliber from stone.

♦

You know this, you've learned this: You need to tap into that spirit, ride along with it, enjoy it, while still maintaining your sense of self. Don't try to swim against the rip tide. Swim sideways, until you're out of it. Or ride it to deeper water, where it will dissipate, or peter out, or take a turn under, or whatever, until you're released from its power, and you're free. Free to swim, free to float, free to speak the way you wish.

A BROWN ALBUM

My FATHER CAME HOME from the hospital yesterday after hip replacement surgery. The same thing that Elizabeth Taylor had. Except my father is seventy-five, has aphasia from stroke, had broken his pelvis and ribs in other falls, has had seizures, and has no money to speak of. He goes to the local hospital for his operations. The reason it was momentous, his coming home, was because my mother had said she wouldn't be able to care for him any longer. After the next episode.

My mother is seventy-three, now overweight and with high blood pressure. She's probably gained fifteen pounds since my father's stroke. She's his primary caregiver. Till death do us part, is her motto regarding marriage.

The morning of my father's stroke I saw the emergency room nurses and doctors go into code blue action twice on my father. It's unnerving when they bring out the Craftsman toolbox, when they bring out the paddles. That was four years ago, the month after my son was born.

My mother felt relief when my father went in this time; she couldn't care for him any longer. Then we thought my father would die. My sister flew in from Northern California, my brother from New York. But my father survived yet again. I call him *vaqueta*, rawhide. He's half the size I remember him from my youth. Three-quarters of his brain is dark in the x-rays, yet when he's "there," he's more there than most unbrain-damaged people I deal with. He's too cogent for my mother to place him in a convalescent home. When he no longer recognizes me, then I'll put him in a home, my mother said.

I had told my father I would be there to take him home from the hospital, once again. But the hospital administrator told my mother he was to be released around ten in the morning. I live in Redlands, my parents in Huntington Beach. I'd have to leave at six in the morning to get there through rush hour traffic, which I could do, but my wife teaches a morning class—she'd have to cancel it. So I talked with my father the night before and asked him if it was okay that I not be there when he was released. My father had taught me to always keep my word. You're nothing, if you don't have a word, my father taught me. Of course he let me off the hook.

The reason it was important for me to be there was that my mother had had a surgical procedure, a colonoscopy, and couldn't do any lifting. That's why we hired a woman to care for my father for a week. But then the nurses at the hospital insisted that they give my father one last meal—they always pamper him because he's such a gentleman. Which made his release time later, after lunch, which made it possible for me to keep my word. And I did.

The woman we hired to help my mother care for him had been to the hospital three days for training by the physical therapist in how to transfer my father from the wheelchair to the bed, to the toilet, etc. My mother said the woman was doing well. She had cared for my father before, when my mother attended one of her various meetings for sewing or crafts. We'd hired I don't know how many women to care for my father, most of them illegal, from the other side, and not many have worked out. A huge difference in culture, for one thing. My parents are very fastidious. And particular. And of course are attached to their things. This woman actually followed orders. She was my age, American, and did only what she was asked to do. Didn't fuck up the washing machine. Didn't break the stove. Didn't take it upon herself to rearrange the kitchen. On and on. The problem, though, is this woman has been ill. Has had a mastectomy. And chemotherapy a while back. She's thin.

At home, my mother and the woman we hired had trouble getting my father into his bed. After fifteen minutes with the seventy-three-year-old wife and the fragile forty-five-year-old woman negotiating with the brain-damaged invalid, I intervened. I muscled my father onto the bed from the wheelchair. Then I exited the room to let the caregivers, my mother and the woman, get him down on the bed. After another prolonged negotiation I intervened yet again to lay my father down—they couldn't get him prone.

Later, we figured that my father was being put on the opposite side of the bed from what he was used to at the hospital.

Sometimes when doing *kata* at the *dojo* the *sensei* has us face a different direction to perform a kata. When you're not very far along in your training this simple change can really throw you off.

I rearranged the furniture in my father's sickroom so that it could replicate that of the hospital's. Then I went to a late show on my way back to Redlands. A John Sayles film. *Lone Star*. Billed (when it got billing) as a drama involving inhabitants of a Texas/Mexico border town. This piqued my interest. I never see films about Chicanos.

Early on in the film the protagonist, the sheriff, Deeds, chastises one of the townspeople for making a disparaging remark about Mexicans. Deeds tells the townsman, who's bemoaning the fact that there will no longer be a white sheriff, a white mayor, or a white majority on the city council, that nineteen out of twenty people here are Mexican. This is what Deeds says to the townsman upset about the "change" in the culture.

Then the film goes on to be about a truly interesting black family, a pretty interesting white family, and a "stock" brown family. The black family has real complexity. The white family has complexity but we've seen it before—I hate my father stuff. The brown family has its roots entirely south of the border, and it seems, every ancestor got his back wet crossing over. Maybe that's how it is in Texas, I don't know. Maybe that's how Sayles's vision works. He's a good writer—the film is great. Sayles doesn't give a shit about pacing, or about moving the story forward for that matter. Much of the film is backstory. And it's all character. Complex characters when looking at black and white families, not so complex when looking at brown families.

What I call the McBean principal.

It goes like this: Nobody's interested enough in good brown characters, so you have to create a character who's not entirely brown—McBean in the wonderful novel *The Adeleta* by Oakley Hall—to deflect attention away from the fact that you're watching a brown character. Hollywood calls this phenomenon "port of entry." What will interest white viewers. Think *Chico and the Man*. Freddie Prince *had* to be paired with Jack Albertson.

I hesitate to criticize Sayles's effort, it's a good film. It was just that I was expecting as much care with Chicanos, as much interest in Chicano culture, as he's shown with African American culture, for example. But his interest or heart doesn't lie there, however. It's still a good film; you don't want to criticize one of the two films that comes out about "your people." But there it is, I expected so much more. I expected complex brown characters. But that's my problem, I suppose.

There's also this. I drove over to South Coast Village to see the film. South Coast Village is right across the street from South Coast Plaza, one of the most affluent shopping centers in the world, I've heard. At one point South Coast Plaza did more dollar volume in sales than any shopping center in the world, or so the story goes. Because it's so upscale.

I worked there many years ago when I did construction for money. We would begin work at eleven at night, work all night, and leave before any shoppers arrived. In those days I worked with a partner whose father had driven tractor for the Segerstrom brothers when they were lima bean farmers, before they built the shopping center on their bean fields.

Across from the cinema is a new Planet Hollywood—I've not been to the area in many years—with palm trees that must reach at least eighty feet into the Orange County ocean night sky. There were a lot of people at the theater on a Tuesday night to see a film about a mythical border town. I think I was the only Latino in attendance.

At the end of the film the Elizabeth Peña character says to Deeds, her lover, Let's forget the Alamo. Critics like this line. I'm ambivalent about it. Things are more complex than that, in my opinion.

◆

They say my paternal grandparents had a horseback courtship. My grandfather was born in 1891 in Piños Altos, New Mexico. His father was Vincent López and his mother was Valentín Barrela. Both sides of the family had land and education but no money. In fact, they say that they were actually married on horseback, a civil ceremony. I can't confirm or deny any of this, however (not yet, at any rate).

When Juan López Barrela met Consuelo Barunda Valdéz, my paternal grandmother, I'm not sure. Juan López Barrela, my paternal grandfather, was raised in New Mexico until he departed for Los Angeles in the early twentieth century.

Consuelo Barunda Valdéz was orphaned at an early age. She was raised by a godmother who took Consuelo to El Paso to work in the family store. Just when my grandmother returned to New Mexico, I don't know. Before her parents died, the family had land. Where it went we don't know. She was married to Juan López Barella in a civil ceremony in New Mexico. Many years later, in the 1940's, they had a Catholic wedding ceremony at St. Anthony's in Los Angeles.

144

My paternal grandfather always had a job, even through the Depression, finally retiring from Union Pacific with the literal gold watch and a pension. My paternal grandmother, Consuelo, worked enough to feed her Christmas saving clubs. She had to do this since Juan controlled the money and drank a lot of whiskey. There's one story which goes: Juan returned home late one Christmas Eve, supposedly with the paycheck for Christmas gifts. He had gotten drunk—he loved whiskey—and had lost his entire check gambling. No Christmas presents, no Christmas dinner. Ergo Consuelo's obsession with Christmas money for the rest of her life. My grandfather was good looking and a sharp dresser. We have photographs of my grandparents on their way to the dances, in which they rode a horse-drawn carriage over wooden bridges into the city.

My father, born to Juan and Consuelo in 1920 in Los Angeles, was the oldest of four children. He did well in school, wasn't any particular trouble, though he participated in the boyhood pranks of city youth. He tells of pulling up the electric car tracks one Halloween with a bunch of other boys. He tells of a confrontation with a particularly fierce cholo who pulled a gun on him. The story goes that my father's friend said, Beto will be happy to fight you, but no guns. Then my father got royally creamed, or so he says. But he wasn't shot. He played violin in the Roosevelt High School Orchestra and he ran varsity track. He'd planned on attending college, but he met my mother, Agripina Estavillo Padilla, when he was a senior in high school. My mother says they met at the time when she'd just purchased her first "grown-up shoes." My father was an older man, one who impressed her by showing up on their first date with a borrowed car—she thought he was rich—candy and flowers. And then World War II broke upon this earth like a nasty, rogue wave, stopping any plans my father might have had for college.

He tried to enlist in the Marines but was turned down because he had a hernia, enlisted in the Navy, and was sent to radio school at the University of Colorado. My mother was pregnant by this time, giving birth to a stillborn child, my first brother. My father was not allowed to return home to console his young wife so he went AWOL, traveling to Los Angeles, where he spent a week with my mother. Upon his return to Colorado, he was placed in the brig, busted down to the lowest rank, and promptly shipped out on tanker duty, the most dangerous of all.

◆

Don Fernando Durán y Chávez had seven sons in the North Kingdom of New Mexico. He also had a daughter, María, who was my mother's great grandmother. María met and married Tiburcio Padilla, who, as all family members had, owned much land. Had no money. One of their children, Frances Padilla Chávez, my mother's mother, was pretty, intelligent, and independent. When she refused to stop seeing the young farmhand from Mexico—you didn't fraternize with the help—she was expelled from the family land. She married that farmhand, Pablo Estavillo Falcón.

Get out your waders here, for this is the one family member who got wet crossing the Rio Grande. Pablo, the story goes, came from the distinguished Falcón family in Mexico.

When an adolescent, sixteen years of age, and attending a military academy, or so the story goes, he confronted a bully who terrorized the boys. Pablo shot him in the face with a gun. Thinking he'd killed the bully, Pablo fled north to the U.S., where he found himself in New Mexico, working on the Padilla spread. And illicitly courting their daughter. Many years later Pablo would find out that he hadn't killed that boy, only stunned him, for there had been blanks in the pistol. Still, this was the catalyst for his river crossing.

They had a tempestuous relationship, with Francis birthing eleven children, my mother the sixth. Agripina Estavillo Padilla. Agripina came from Agripina Falcón, the Falcón matriarch.

They too headed to Los Angeles in the early twentieth century. Frances made use of her knowledge of herbs and curing, and thus was known as a *curandera*. She induced labor to terminate unwanted pregnancies with herbs, and virtually practiced medicine, my mother says. Frances made do with what she could provide; Pablo did not work steadily. My mother likes to say her mother was a hippie before her time. I think of her as a free spirit.

During my mother's childhood the family moved back and forth between New Mexico and Los Angeles. On one of these trips my grandmother sold alcohol on a reservation—my mother was born on a reservation—an illegal act. The problem was that when the men became drunk, they wanted more whiskey, and Frances had no more. There was a big stink over this , from every side. On another trip, when my mother was a juvenile, she was badly burned in a kitchen grease fire. She suffered third degree burns on her torso, was hospitalized, and left behind. My grandmother was in a hurry to move on. My mother was subsequently placed in an orphanage, where she remained until her father took her out.

My mother was terribly interested in getting an education and had to fight with her mother in order to attend school. Frances needed help with the younger children. Once, my mother went to school in the morning. When she returned in the afternoon, her family had moved, not even bothering to inform her! An older brother came in the evening to retrieve his little sister. Still, my mother did well in school, marrying right before her graduation, but graduating just the same.

◆

Robert Lopez, my father, had dropped the second last name and the accent above the -ó, and Aggie, what my mother called herself, dropping the -ripina off her first name and making it perky with the addition of -gie, had four children. I was the second. Actually there were five. The first was stillborn. The second died of AIDS at forty-one years of age. Now there are three children. The second (or third) born is a professor of English and writes. The third (or fourth) born is working on her Ph.D., works in Silicon Valley, and lives in a house worth over half-a-million dollars. The fourth (or fifth) born works in NYC as a VP for a visual merchandise company.

There may be a few felons in my family, I don't know, but if there are they are not the norm. More accurately, there are a number of Ph.D.s, a number of lawyers, college professors, a U.S. judge, Postal Service workers, high school teachers, administrators, mechanics, construction workers, military personnel, and, yes, even a few cholos and cholas.

♦

Sometime last summer, before my father had broken his hip and almost died for the sixth time, I took my mother to Los Angeles for a combined 100th and 80th birthday party. One of my uncles was turning eighty. His mother was one-hundred. This particular uncle had married into the family. My mother hired a woman—the one who was with us when we brought my father home—to care for my father while we were gone. I had wanted to bring my son, for I remember those gatherings of my youth: christenings, weddings, birthdays, and holidays, running wild with cousins whom I wouldn't see again for many years, if at all. I thought my son might enjoy some aspects of playing with relatives too. But I had to drive to Huntington Beach from Redlands, sixty miles, then drive thirty miles to Los Angeles, and then do the reverse after the party. My four-year old doesn't travel that well. Hell, I don't either.

At the gathering there were five generations of my family represented. It was held in the backyard of one of my cousins, a woman who is divorced, raised her children with help from their father, and used to fly small airplanes when she was younger. The party was held in my cousin's backyard. It had been hot lately, but this day there was a tiny breeze working its way from the ocean. And my cousin had tent-like structures in the backyard, under the trees, further cooling the guests. There were a lot of people, the backyard full. A buffet was served, Mexican food, naturally, and some boys were serving wine and beer out of coolers for tips.

I'd not been to one of these things in many years. I introduced myself to a man I thought was a cousin, and he was. He name was Tiger. How do you do, Mr. Tiger. He was a tiger, tiger tattoos on his arms. Big guy, looked like a Samoan, but he was family. I looked over the gathering, and saw little old ladies with cross tattoos in the fleshy parts of their hands, and I saw dressed for success leisure outfits on younger professionals, and I saw children running around throwing balls. The ones I couldn't take my eyes off were the two young women with the painted lips, the lips that looked as if they were tattooed in dark blood. The girls were knockdown beautiful. One was probably seventeen, with a three-month-old child. She and her friend were at the end of the table where my uncles sat with their wives. I sat with my uncles; one's a retired school principal, the other a retired builder, and they began telling me stories of the old days. That's why I sit with them.

After a time a young man, short, with a military haircut, came over and introduced himself to me. I thought he was married to the young woman with the baby. Faux pas! He was her father, the baby was his granddaughter. The young woman was my second cousin, the baby my third. The reason this cousin by marriage introduced himself to me was that he was soon to retire from the army, and was taking writing classes at a community college, and he wanted to talk with me about writing. He wanted to be a writer after his retirement. It brought to mind my graduate school professor, the one who told my wife to stay away from me, my wife's surrogate father, who used to rant in class about when he retired from his position at UC, when he retired as a writer, he was going to take up brain surgery. Either that or become a concert pianist. What he used to say.

I spoke with this man my age, who cornered me for a long time. He wanted to know the secret of writing. I told him it was hard work, that it took a lot of discipline, that you had to fill up a whole bunch of pages. He didn't know how to get started, he told me. We sat there in my cousin's backyard, drinking ice-cold beer, eating lovely food, with the chatter of family, loved ones, people who look pretty much the same as you do, though you don't know their names, not all of them, and still, he wanted me to impart some sort of secret code to him. An edge to get him writing.

I remembered what my older brother had told me not long before his death, when I was floundering about, not really admitting what it was exactly I wished to do. My brother told me, First, you take out a little pencil. Then you get yourself some *papeles*, and you begin writing. That's it. Just start writing. What my brother told me.

PATHOS, BATHOS, AND MEXIPHOBIA

Let's cut to the chase. Three chases, actually. Two high-speed police pursuits and a metaphorical one. The police pursuits embody pathos and bathos. The metaphorical chase is painful and enlightening, possibly liberating.

The chase: I'm an American of Mexican descent. That's what my father taught me to say. Not Mexican. Not Chicano. Not Spanish. Not Hispanic. American. Of Mexican descent. I'm an American citizen. Rodney King is an American citizen. Alicia Sotero Vásquez and Adrián Flores Martínez are Mexican citizens.

Why did my father coach me on what to say? Why must I announce my background? Because of my last name, which you would notice before you read this, if you read it at all. Let's cut to the chase. I'm a "guest" or foreigner here, *xeno*. In spite of the fact that my father explicitly told me I'm an American. What's your nationality? Are you Spanish? You're not like them. All these things have been asked or said to me.

First chase, metaphorical chase: there is a racial hierarchy in the United States, as I've previously stated.

Always has been, always will be, unless we actually begin space travel in earnest, because in outer space, traveling away from earth, everyone could be called earthlings.

The racial hierarchy. Norse sailors come to North America. Return home. Don't leave much in the way of remnants. English settle New England. They are the guests but treat the aboriginal people as "other" and drive them inland. As do French and Spanish colonizers. All the colonists stake out their turf. Aborigines not welcome. Finally, after the dust settles after the French Indian Wars, The Revolutionary War, the War of 1812, the Mexican American War, the Monroe Doctrine, and thousands and thousands of local skirmishes, Mexicans, Spanish, French, British, and native Americans are vanquished. English is the spoken language of the country. My language.

There was a high-speed pursuit by Riverside County Sheriff deputies of a pickup truck carrying suspected illegal immigrants . It went on for eighty miles. Attorneys for the police say that the suspected illegal immigrants pelted police with beer bottles and debris from the back of the truck. The driver of the pickup allegedly tried to ram other cars on the freeway to create a diversion for officers giving chase. When the driver of the pickup truck finally stopped, everyone ran. Except for two people. A man and a woman.

The Civil War was supposedly fought over the moral issue of slavery. Mortar is used to keep the bricks apart. The Civil War was fought over the *taxation* of slavery.

The drop of blood principle. If you have one drop of colored blood, you're colored. Unless you don't look colored. Rodney King looks colored. Alicia Sotero Vásquez and Adrián Flores Martínez look colored. More than a drop of blood for those guys. I've been asked, Isn't your mother white? This by a friend with whom I escaped stabbing at the hands of Hawaiians because we were xeno on their island. It was an attempt by my friend to elevate me in status. We could have lost our lives that night. Sorry, my mother's name is Agripina Estavillo. Agripina is from the Roman (Agrippina). Estavillo is Mexican.

Still, I might be able to cheat the one drop rule. Probably not, however. My son, though, will have no problem doing so. He's what Rudolfo Anaya calls in his novel, *Alburquerque*, the "new mestizo." My son has blue eyes. Sandy brown hair. *Güero* in Spanish. Fair. Takes after his mother.

The performance artist and MacArthur Fellow Gómez Peña was having lunch with his ex-wife, a professor of Comparative Literature at UC San Diego, and their child. They told their child they would buy him some toys after the meal. There had been a kidnapping in the San Diego area. Illegal immigrants (read Mexicans) were suspected of the crime. Two other diners overheard Gómez Peña and his ex-wife talking to their child. They called the police. The SWAT team descended on the MacArthur Fellow, arresting him.

Rodney King led police on a high-speed pursuit. When it was over he wouldn't comply with the officers' orders. He was beaten. On videotape. Alicia Sotero Vásquez and Adrián Flores Martínez were involved in a high-speed freeway pursuit. When it was over they didn't comply with the officers' orders. They were beaten. On videotape. Zsa Zsa Gabor was pulled over by a Beverly Hills police officer. She wouldn't comply with his orders. She slapped the officer. No high speed chase. No videotape. No beating. Rodney King was arrested. Alicia Sotero Vásquez and Adrián Flores Martínez were arrested. Zsa Zsa Gabor was arrested.

Rodney King was quoted in the newspaper the day after

his arrest as saying: I took my beating like a man. He knew the hierarchical order.

As I've said, I drive a long distance to my place of employment. I listened to the first Rodney King beating trial while commuting. The Simi Valley trial, the one before the riots. Stacey Koon testified that he saved Rodney King's life that night because he could have ordered deadly force under such conditions. Instead they beat Rodney King in order to arrest him. No guns. Only batons. They would have been well within their rights to draw their guns, Stacey Koon said. He believed this. I believed him. He knew the hierarchy.

When I was a child there was a time before my peers grew, before adolescence, when I was the largest and the quickest. I was good in sports—baseball, football, basketball. Once when trying out for a football team the coach, who thought I was the best athlete on the field and who liked me, told me a joke. He said there was a nigger who wanted to be on a team. Nobody wanted the nigger on their team and the coach didn't know what to do. During the tryout the nigger broke free and was running for a touchdown, my coach told me. The coach in the joke, my coach said, started yelling, Look at that Mexican run! I wondered even at the time why this grown man was telling me such an offensive "joke." To put me in my place? To bond with me, telling me that I was better than a "nigger"? Or to make me aware of the hierarchy?

I have a friend and colleague who's a linguist. Guillermo Bartelt's field is Native American languages. My friend says that assimilation was never intended to apply to dark people. It was a description appropriate to what occurred after Northern Europeans lived a generation or two in the United States. Northern Europeans come from different countries with different languages. But everyone speaks English after a time. That is what assimilation means, my friend told me. Assimilation doesn't apply to African or southern European or Asian people. Or American aborigines. Guillermo Bartelt said. The linguist.

Some friends of mine stayed a time in Provence. They had guests over for dinner one night. An English couple and an American couple. The American woman, the guest of my friends, was dark. At some point during the evening the British woman said to the American woman, I knew you were American but I didn't know you were foreign. British woman to American woman.

My friend the linguist said that it was really about competition between England and Spain for territory in the new world. It wasn't a result of the Mexican American War, though this inflamed emotions. It really went back to the defeat of the Spanish Armada. There had been a distrust between the English and Spanish which predated the colonization of America, Guillermo Bartelt said. The hierarchy.

All this past week on the Discovery Channel a show called *Wild Discovery* has shown game preserves in Russia. My four-year old loves animals, komodo dragons in particular. He saw komodo dragons last week on a game preserve in Indonesia. After one of the episodes my wife remarked, we don't often think of anyone other than Americans when thinking of animal preservation. We think we're the keepers of all species, I thought.

We don't like to think of ourselves as having deep-rooted biases against cultures and races. When Arabs and Jews fight we say they've been doing it for centuries. When Muslims and Christians fight we say they've been at odds for centuries. When civil war flares in Asia we say they've been fighting forever. Same with Africa. Same with Latin America.

I'm working on a novel that addresses what it's like being of Mexican (New Mexican, actually) descent in California. That is why I was talking with Guillermo Bartelt. I want to coin a term, I told him, that would capture the disregard for an entire culture. I want to come up with a word or phrase, such as "anti-Semitism," that would have universal meaning. My friend said that for anti-Semitism this wasn't entirely the case. He said the term refers to all speakers of Arabic languages. How can an Arab be against himself? as an Arab might respond to the term. That's all well and good, I replied, but the only denotation in a contemporary context for anti-Semitism is hatred against Jews. He agreed. He couldn't come up with a term for me to describe my book.

Then he called a few days later with the word: *Mexiphobia*. We tossed it around, but I wasn't sold that it captured the insidious institutional aspect of the bias against Mexicans in California. He argued that *phobia* did address the unreasonable and irrational fears many people speak of publicly and participate in privately when dealing with Mexicans or people of Mexican descent.

Pathos: Human beating human. Armed, baton-wielding human being beating unarmed non-resisting human being. On videotape.

There are any number of monolithic belief systems operating in America. Liberal, Conservative, Democratic, Republican, Black, Brown, Red, Yellow, White Supremacist, Feminist, Gay, Lesbian, Law Enforcement, Civil Rights,

Christian, Conservation, Animal Rights, etc. The people who work within the belief systems usually will embrace anyone who thinks as they do. None of the realms of the monolithic belief systems are mutually exclusive. You can use the black regent who truly believes he made it on his own as a front man to end Affirmative Action in California.

The monolithic belief systems many times keep people from engaging in dialog. Law Enforcement advocates will back their men; black rights advocates will back their men; Chicano rights activists will back their people. Particularly with regard to volatile and emotional media events. O.J. Simpson. Rodney King. Bernard Goetz. William Masters. Alicia Sotero Vásquez and Adrián Flores Martínez.

After the Riverside beating Chicano-rights advocates chided a law professor who said that legally there weren't many similarities between the Rodney King beating and the Alicia Sotero Vásquez/Adrián Flores Martínez beating. The Rodney King beating was videotaped. Officers participating in the beating didn't know they were being filmed. Rodney King is an American citizen. Alicia Sotero Vásquez and Adrián Flores Martínez are Mexican citizens. Officers involved in the beating knew they were videotaped (or did they?). There's also an audiotape of the incident. A CHP officer left his tape recorder running at the time of the arrests.

As an adolescent I went surfing with friends at a place called Trestles. On Camp Pendleton. U.S. Government property. You had to trespass to get to the water. You'd be dropped off in the dirt at a freeway underpass, cross the I 5—the same freeway that goes to the Mexico border—trek through a "jungle," paddle across a pond, and walk across white sand to the most pristine surf break you'll ever see. It was uncrowded in those days.

After surfing all day, on the walk back to the pickup point, we were confronted by MPs. Too tired to run, we stopped. We were told that what we were doing was illegal. We gave phony names to the MPs. Well, not phony, just not our real names. The names of famous surfers. Name? Duke Kahanamoku. Name? Greg Knoll. Name? Dewey Weber. We couldn't hold back our giggles. Surely the MPs would know that the scrawny adolescents before them weren't world-famous surfers. The MPs were from Louisiana and Oklahoma and Indiana. They didn't know about surfing.

Upon her arrest Alicia Sotero Vásquez gave her name as Leticia González González. Adrián Flores Martínez said his name was Enrique Funes Flores. They either knew they were trespassing or knew the hierarchy or knew both.

I train *shito-ryu* style karate. Sometimes during *kumite* I must spar with women. One night after training I told my partner I was at a disadvantage when working with her. Her response was, Of course. It runs counter to everything you've been taught, she said. You don't hit women, I was taught.

Ernest Gaines, the superb fiction writer, often confronts in his fiction the theme of the black man not protecting his women. The white man did, Gaines writes. Protect his women. So much so that a black man could be lynched for looking at a white women, Gaines writes.

Pathos: Alicia Sotero Vásquez clubbed as she tries to emerge from the truck. Alicia Sotero Vásquez grabbed by her long hair and thrown to the ground while being clubbed. Alicia Sotero Vásquez slammed against the hood of the pickup truck. Offering no resistance. None.

159

The pickup truck carrying the at the time suspected illegal immigrants (after the chase and capture and arrests of the suspects we learned indeed they were entering the United States illegally, and they were Mexican citizens) leads police officers on an eighty-mile freeway chase. The camper shell disintegrates and pieces fall around other motorists while police follow the truck. When it stops all the cowards run. The police give chase.

Except Alicia Sotero Vásquez and Adrián Flores Martínez don't run. Alicia Sotero Vasquez said from her hospital bed that she did nothing wrong. She only came here to work. Did she not run because she felt she did nothing wrong or did she have trouble getting out of the pickup truck? Adrián Flores Martínez came around the side of the pickup, or so it appeared on videotape, to help his girlfriend exit the truck. He was greeted with blows from a policeman's baton.

Only officers Kurt Franklin and Tracy Watson know in their hearts whether or not they felt threatened by the non-fleeing man and woman. Only they know their motivations, their intentions. Only they know whether or not their actions constituted bravery or cowardice. Only those two officers. Kurt Franklin and Tracy Watson.

Mahandas Gandhi said: Everybody is right from his own standpoint, but it is not impossible that everybody is wrong.

Proponents of the monolithic belief systems have now taken over the event, appropriating it for their particular agendas. Whatever happens legally, you will still maintain your own take on the event, depending upon which "monolith" you subscribe to.

You've heard all the rhetoric about how California was part of Mexico and people from Mexico feel they can come to California because it was formerly their country. You've heard that California is part of the spiritual homeland for Chicanos. But you don't want to hear these things. You're bored with these arguments. You're even bored with the argument that there was a government sanctioned program called the Bracero Program which allowed Mexicans into the state legally to pick crops. You're really bored with the argument that Mexicans *do* get work when they come here. You only know the economy is sputtering.

The scholar Rodolfo Acuña says this anti-Mexican sentiment is historical and as regular as any ocean tide. California economy good, Mexicans "allowed" in to perform non-skilled labor. California economy falters, close the border. Migrant workers sí, migrant workers no.

A writer to the Letters section of the *Los Angeles Times* has written: If the truck had been carrying Canadians, a Canadian woman would not have been clubbed. Imagine a dilapidated pickup truck full of border crashing Zsa Zsa Gabors. Imagine all the Zsa Zsa Gabors, upon the truck stopping, slapping Kurt Franklin and Tracy Watson. Imagine that.

Liberation: I no longer use the term racism. It's gone the way of overused and meaningless terms such as have a good day and politically correct. My eyes glaze over when someone mentions P.C. Same with the taunt, you're a racist. Auto pilot. Did. Did not. Did so. Didn't.

Cut to the chase. We're all Race Aware in the United States. It's just a fact of life. The hierarchy. Can we all please stop denying this fact? It's part of the fabric of American culture. Always has been.

We are race aware in this country. Mexiphobia exists.

Mexiphobia: Day workers handcuffed to a fence by a store owner. And then paper bags placed over their heads. Clowns drawn on one side of the bag, the non-idiomatic words "no mas aqui" on the other side. Handcuffed to a fence. By a store owner. Mexican day laborers. Mexican man hit by a hit and run driver. He lies in the median for three days. Commuters and pedestrians see him in the middle of the road, in the median, but do nothing. A store owner sees the man everyday. Thought he was another wetback sleeping in the bushes. CHP officer finally stops to investigate. Three days later. During the Los Angeles riots a Mexican man is beaten, stripped from the waist down, his genitalia spray painted. William Masters, the citizen who confronted other citizens spray painting a freeway underpass at one in the morning, shot both of them during the confrontation, killing the eighteen-year old. William Masters said they were "Mexican skinheads."

Mexiphobia exists.

Because I say Mexiphobia exists doesn't mean I'm anti-law. Because I say Alicia Sotero Vásquez and Adrián Flores Martínez were beaten by police officers doesn't mean I'm anti-police. Of course Alicia Sotero Vásquez, Adrián Flores Martínez, et al, shouldn't have been in this country illegally. Of course the driver of the pickup truck should have stopped when confronted first by Border Patrol agents and later by local law enforcement agencies. Of course the driver of the pickup truck and the occupants should not have endangered other motorists and police officers by being in the country illegally and then attempting to flee when caught. Of course the migrants in the pickup truck should not have run when the truck stopped. Of course Alicia

Sotero Vásquez and Adrián Flores Martínez should have hit the deck when ordered to do so. Of course I'm aware of the fact that there are thousands of police/citizen interactions on a daily basis in which force is not used. Of course I would have been outraged had all the occupants of the pickup truck turned on the three police officers and beaten them. Of course I grieve for the officers slain in the line of duty—the ultimate act of bravery—and for their families and colleagues. All of this should go without saying. But I must say it. It's not an either/or issue. For 'em or ag'in 'em. If I say police should not have clubbed the non-resisting woman, it doesn't mean I'm for illegal immigration. All I'm saying is this. Alicia Sotero Vásquez and Adrián Flores Martínez should not have been beaten. That's all.

Further liberation: Viktor Frankl said in his book *Man's Search for Meaning,* All we can control is our response to the acts of indecent people. Gandhi, King and Chavez would have been proud of Alicia Sotero Vásquez and Adrián Flores Martínez. For in the *satyagraha* tradition, they stood their ground. They offered no resistance. They made no threats. Their non-violence overcame their tormentors' aggression, making them victorious in the encounter, making them righteous for the moment, at least.

Personal liberation: My people have lived in "America" for at least as long as any DAR member. I'm an American of Mexican descent. New Mexican. A Chicano. A product of Spanish and Indian blood. Mestizo. Mexican. American.

WHAT I'VE LEARNED

THE U.S. MARINE CORPS wishes to build officers' housing above Cotton's Point on Camp Pendelton. Cotton's Point is the common name for San Mateo Point. I surfed there in my youth. I've walked down the beach, all the way past Cotton's to Upper Trestles, where I surfed with my friends unmolested, the only ones in the water on an early spring south swell, the tide receding. As an adolescent before I realized what a big deal the U.S. Presidency was, I tried to sneak into Cotton's Point when Nixon was at the Western White House. Not a chance. Police and Secret Service littered the streets like so much beach trash—I couldn't get close enough to even attempt the walk.

I spent my afternoon yesterday getting shirts made for my friend, fellow writer Ricardo Means Ybarra, and me. Another friend, the poet Ben Saltman, a colleague of mine, had introduced us. Ricardo is a tile setter. I worked for years building houses, even getting a General Contractor's License. Ricardo and I have that in common, building. And this: writing. He's published numerous poems, I've published short stories and essays. He's published two novels, *The Pink Rosary* and *Brotherhood of Dolphins*, though both with small presses. At Ricardo's urging, I am now with his

164

agent, who's trying to sell my novel, *The Baja Sky*. Ricardo and I commiserate often about what a sorry-ass state of affairs publishing is in. Specially if you're Latino. That's why I was getting T-shirts made. We're starting our own literary club—The Chicano Surfing Association. We have that in common as well, the surfing. I grew up in Huntington Beach, and surfing was a major part of my adolescence. Ricardo grew up in Echo Park, surfed, lives in Malibu, and still surfs. I thought he'd get a detective book *series* from *Brotherhood of Dolphins*. It has all the elements of good detective fiction. I read drafts of Ricardo's manuscripts, offering suggestions. He critiques my fiction, helping me to revise. We feel completely powerless and cast adrift vis-à-vis the literary world, hence The Chicano Surfing Association.

I took from the back of the *Los Angeles Times Magazine* an ad for Colombian coffee, put out by the Colombian Coffee Growers Association. It's a color picture of what looks like a fifteen-foot day at Sunset Beach, the big peak breaking right, with Juan Valdez and his burro on a surfboard. Underneath it says: *Grab Life by the beans.*—Juan Valdez.

On the front of the T-shirt I have an image of the *calenderio del sol*, the Aztec sun calendar. I have a piece of silver jewelry of the sun stone that my wife gave me. It's gold in the middle. On the T-shirt around the sun stone are the words: Chicano Surfing Association. The font is called Corona. An inside joke. I had all these things made into a heat transfer so they could be put on the T-shirts.

I belong to Surfrider Foundation. The San Diego Chapter in Encinitas. Even though I've never attended a meeting. My wife and son and I vacation at Moonlight Beach in July or August for a week, and my son calls where we stay "the little beach house." My son loves the ocean. His middle name is Delfín. I love dolphins.

Ever since I had a transcendental experience way down in Baja California, when I was fifteen-years old and surfing at a spot no one had ever surfed before, and the waves were huge, not unlike the one Juan Valdez and his burro are riding. In the afternoon a school of dolphins appeared in the cove. They surfed with us, and knocked us off our boards, and there were a few babies with the team, and I've never experienced a communion with water and nature like that since. The next day the cove was shrouded in fog and we couldn't see the waves, only hear them crashing on the reef, and the dolphins were gone.

I'm ambivalent about the officer's housing at Cotton's Point. I surfed Doheny and Dana Point before the breakwater went in. No more waves now. There will still be waves at Cotton's Point.

During the Vietnam War I was prepared to refuse induction. Go to prison. I even had to move from Oregon, where I was living at the time, in order to refuse induction at the draft board where I registered. My parents hired a lawyer for me; to pay them back I got a job working with my father at Mead Packaging in Buena Park, where he worked. I had to pass a physical examination in order to be hired. My father was a printer, the foreman at that time, though he was soon to be taken in at the management level. He also served in the U.S. Navy during World War II. Still, he supported my decision not to serve in Vietnam. I claimed to be a conscientious objector, but now know this was not the case. My decision was a selective refusal, something the draft laws don't allow for. When the results of my back x-rays came in, my father's company wouldn't hire me. I have a condition in my spine called spondylolysis. Which means one of the vertebrae in my lower back is broken and it shifts capriciously from time to time, causing incredible back pain, cutting off blood circulation to my leg, and in general making my life miserable. The military wouldn't take me, even had I wanted to go, with a condition such as I had. Though they wouldn't have bothered with x-rays, had I not discovered the condition on my own.

I'm a patriot. I was willing to go to jail for my country.

Ricardo got out of the draft by simply going back and forth between California and Colorado. They'd send him his draft notice, he'd move on, the notice would get returned. They'd give him an extension. I knew a guy who got hold of his entire draft file. He threw it away, thereby not existing any longer. I knew of guys who had anal sex so they could claim they were homosexual and not be drafted. I knew a guy who drove a nail in the bottom of his foot to get a draft extension.

And this: Steve I coming down to Bolsa Chica, which is between Huntington Beach and Seal Beach, where we surfed, after his tour of duty, telling us not to go no matter what. Steve I, who was a well-decorated soldier and who let us feel the metal shrapnel still imbedded in his chest and legs and who no longer wished to surf. Steve I, lecturing us on the beach. There's no reason for you to go, Steve I said.

I was morally opposed to the Vietnam War. And willing to pay the price for my conviction. No running away. Except I wouldn't have done that well in prison, I don't think. I would have been incarcerated at the federal penitentiary at Terminal Island in Los Angeles Harbor. For at least three years. In Oregon I would've done six months planting trees on the Tillamook Burn. But they changed horses in the race. To prevent young men from doing their time in a state where sentiment was against the war, the Nixon White House, by presidential decree, stated that one must refuse induction at the place where one originally registered for the draft. I registered for the draft in Orange County, California. The home of Prop 187. When I appeared before the men at my interview about claiming conscientious objector status I told them I would not fight. They asked me what I would do if confronted with Hitler. I cannot answer that, I said, it's hypothetical. I'm not confronted with Hitler, I said, I'm confronted with an immoral war. I don't believe in war, I told them. One of the draft board members wished me luck. He meant it. I thought this a good sign, that the men believed I was a man of conviction, that I'd won them over. I was classified 1A: I'm Chicano.

This is why I'm ambivalent about the officers' housing at Cotton's Point: These men, these Marines, have dedicated their lives to protecting our country. Some have seen action, some haven't. Still, if ordered, they'll go. They're Marines. They will fight, follow orders. So why can't they also enjoy the pristine waves at Cotton's Point the way I did in my youth? Why can't they have a place of beauty and calmness where they might spend time with their families? A "little beach house," in other words.

I know I shouldn't be ambivalent about this issue. I'm firmly committed to keeping the environment in its natural state as much as possible. Yet I'm also aware of the function of the military, even though I don't believe in war.

Many years ago I traveled around Europe by train. Often-times at frontier crossings you'd show the border guard your American passport and they'd wave you through without even looking at it. That's some power, in my opinion. And I've been the recipient of that power. And those officers who want to live above Cotton's Point are part of the reason for that power, the reason for the deferential treatment shown to me by officials from other countries. I know I'm supposed to be for the environment, and I am.

I'm a graduate from the writing program at UC Irvine. A number of people I studied with have become full-time writers, a book out every two years or so. Three of the males who were in my class of six students have eight books out among them. They have made names for themselves. I have written three books, none of them published.

The two women with whom I studied in the program haven't published any books either. In fact, I've not seen anything in print with their names. I doubt if they've seen my publications. Why do those three guys have eight published books while the three other writers who were also deemed talented have none?

A most complex issue. Having to do with business, with trends, with connections, with the writing itself, maybe even with karma.

But I know this much: My market for selling a book is extremely limited—I write about middle-class people with Latino names. There are certain expectations editors have about people with Latino last names. When I wrote a story about a guy who was going to jail, every editor who saw it loved it. It was published in an important short story anthology. The Chicano who would go to jail. Embraced by publishing.

I won't write that story any longer. I don't care to write about the Chicano gang member. I care about the Chicano overachiever who is making inroads in areas formally closed to Chicanos. I care, for example, about the Latina activist concerned about the proliferation of nuclear power. She to me is infinitely more interesting than the gang member.

It's difficult for any artist to deal with the convergence of art and commerce. It's not personal, it's business. I can make the above statement after years of rejection. After hitting doors, kicking chairs, laughing, weeping, howling, meditating upon the rejection. After alcohol, cocaine, prozac and therapy. (The therapist asked me why I couldn't publish in Mexico?)

So I keep writing, it's what I do.

And I'm ambivalent about the Marine officers at Cotton's Point.

Once when I was in the eleventh grade I ditched school with some friends and we went surfing at Trestles. Trestles is named for the train trestle that overlooks the reef at San Mateo Point and beyond. The surf breaks on U.S. Government property. As stated earlier, you have to sneak in to surf there. At least in those days you did.

The waves were small that day I ditched school with my friends. About three to four feet, the waves were. But they had that Trestles long ride. We surfed Uppers, which is between Cotton's Point and Lowers.

In the afternoon some Marines in fatigues arrived on the beach in Jeeps. They yelled at us through loudspeakers to get out of the water. We ignored them. When one of the guys I was with lost his board—we'd not heard of leashes—it went into shallow water in toward shore. One of the Marines ran into the surf in order to get my friend's board. Another guy surfing with us rode a wave all the way in, grabbed the loose surfboard, and paddled it out to its owner before the Marine could get it.

This made the Marines on the beach furious.

Some of the guys I surfed with began flipping off the Marines.

They left.

A short time later they returned with inflatable rafts. Each raft held four to six Marines. They began chasing us in the gentle waves, sometimes getting close. One of the guys I surfed with began taunting those Marines. He would let them get right behind his board and then take off on a wave, leaving the raft far behind.

It wasn't that difficult to outmaneuver the rafted Marines by surfing. Inside, where the whitewater was, they'd capsize. So we just played cat and mouse with them until they were too tired to chase us any longer.

Except they stayed on the beach. And had the last laugh—we had to paddle all the way to the north of Cotton's Point, off the Marine base, to exit the surf. A very long paddle.

Another time two friends and I were surprised by Marines as we walked back to our car after surfing all day. They confiscated our boards, and my father had to take time off work, accompanying me to the Provost Marshall's office on Camp Pendleton.

After the war, my father, as a reward for his twenty-seven months continuous duty in the Pacific during World War II, was given shore duty at Camp Pendleton. He and my mother lived off-base in Fallbrook. It was here during this time that my parents met the Bishops, Jack and Imelda. Jack Bishop: I'm his namesake. He was also a Navy man, had seen extensive action in the Pacific, and like my father, was rewarded with shore duty at Camp Pendleton. They were MPs. Working under the Provost Marshall's office. My parents were from Boyle Heights in East Los Angeles. The Bishops were from Manhattan Beach. Their families owned businesses and beach houses. My memories of early childhood consist of playing on the sand at Manhattan Beach, and having barbecues in the afternoons, and running wild while the parents drank themselves into happiness. It had been a long war.

When my father took me to get my board, the Provost Marshall gave me a tongue lashing. My father had been an MP at this very same base. But he said nothing to the Provost Marshall. When we closed the door to the office, after my tongue lashing, all my father said was, Asshole. He meant the Provost Marshall. He also told me not to surf there any longer. I did surf there again, though I was never caught. My father told me many years later that I would do fine in battle. This had a liberating effect on me and helped me to make my anti-Vietnam War decision.

I suppose I'm ambivalent about the Marine housing at Cotton's Point because I have such a history with the area. Maybe because I was forever changed by the prospect of going to prison. Or maybe I've got all these things confused in my memory

◆

My *sensei* often says that his *sensei* said, Perhaps the world is as it should be.

The reason I have a *sensei* is because I began to study martial arts at age forty. I wanted to do something physical, because I mostly sat around reading and writing. I wished to pursue an endeavor in which you were judged according to your ability, not market or business caprice.

I have obtained the rank of *shodan* in the Zen Bei Butokokai. My *sensei* tells me that now he can begin to teach me karate. I trained hard to reach my rank, and in some respects it was harder than graduate school. I thoroughly enjoy a system which makes me compete against myself. A system in which I am my own worst enemy, a system in which I am my own opponent.

How do I reconcile my study of martial arts with my opposition to war? Easy. The martial arts teach that violence in immoral.

I balance the revelation that things are as they should be with the thought of a cosmic jester. My mother's mother was a *curandera* in New Mexico. I have friends who are psychic, and I sometimes use divination, which is often accurate. I am committed to using intuitive powers existing in me and in all of us. I listen to my intuition, though this is a skill I have developed only later in life, for we are taught to abandon our intuition in favor of scientific "fact."

I often have prescient dreams. Virtually every major event in my life I've dreamed before it happened. I can't always access the dream at the appropriate time, however, thus I'm unable to incorporate the prescient quality of it into my intuition in order to give me a less rocky ride.

An acquaintance was visited in a dream by an ex-husband who was deceased. The ex-husband didn't know me. He told the acquaintance, in the dream, that I would have a son who was "half-Mexican."

The above dream may be dismissed quite easily. Except for me there is one striking detail: Are there racial concerns on the "other side"? Is there a racial hierarchy even in the afterlife?

I know there are no Mexicans in outer space. Maybe one has been on Star Trek after all these years, I don't know. The only reason the television series even comes to mind is because my son, the "half-Mexican," watched the show for a time when he was a toddler.

A recent study pointed out the fact that Latinos are portrayed on television 1% of the airtime. The study also pointed out that most of the portrayals are stereotypical. The number, one percent, was down from the 1950s when 3% of the airtime was devoted to Latinos.

Latinos are the second largest racial minority in the United States, projected to become the largest. Latinos already comprise over 50% of the population of Los Angeles. Los Angeles has never had a Latino mayor or police chief. California has never had a Latino governor, not since it became part of the Union.

I was born on the second day of the second month in the second part of the twentieth century. I was the second son.

◆

I've taken to giving to panhandlers as my form of tithing. That and donating household items to Community Assistance, an organization housed in an old church. The program gives directly to needy people. I see them in line waiting for food and clothing and bedding when I drop off our discards at the old church. I know you're not supposed to give to the needy; the reasoning is that you're only contributing to their problems. But I've developed a mighty phobia for administrators since working for a huge bureaucracy. I will not support mid-level management. The Salvation Army is primarily administered by volunteers. The Catholic Archdiocese of Los Angeles is run by approximately 900 staffers. The L.A. Unified School District has about ten times that amount proportionally of administrators to students. My experience has been that the administrators create superfluous work to justify their jobs and salaries. Hence my penchant for giving directly to those I deem needy, thereby circumventing administration.

I spent a lot of time in Ensenada in Baja California, Mexico. My parents and I had a place on the beach. One summer I worked on my MFA thesis, a novel. I would often go into town in the evenings to eat and relax. I would talk with local people. There were always beggars in the streets, sometimes in the restaurants and bars. The local people from Ensenada told me that the beggars, small, dark, Indian-looking women with tiny babies who sometimes suckled while the women begged, were brought in by unscrupulous ringleaders for the particularly sad and pathetic demeanor these women had. Do not give the beggars money, I was told. But I always gave them money. Even if it was a scam, how much money could they be making?

♦

I took my son to the market the other day. My wife was in Florida, visiting her mother, and my son and I were alone, holding down the fort, "baching" it. For four days. My mother came out and spent one night with us. After she left, a Sunday afternoon, I ran errands with my son. I was exhausted yet in a celebratory mood; my wife would return the next day. My son and I went to Stater Brothers. They have those weird top-loading carts where the front flops open so the checker can remove the groceries. My son has never ridden in the part of the cart where you put your groceries, only in the "designated seat."

I put him in the seat, but he was in his cat persona and meowing and insisted that he be allowed to crawl around like a cat in the cart. I was exhausted—it was easier to let him ride where he shouldn't. I reached behind me to get my checkbook out of my backpocket; I heard a metal clank; I saw my son falling headfirst onto the linoleum-covered concrete. He hit on his forehead. His head stuck on the floor for just a second, long enough for his body to bend at his neck, and then collapse around him.

A larger person would have broken his neck. The blow to the head could have caused brain damage, and that was my thought as I rushed to him, sweeping him off the floor. He was crying, a good thing, I found out later. And he didn't vomit or get nauseated. And his pupils were the same size, one not larger than the other. He didn't lose consciousness. But I had to observe him for twenty-four hours, alone, thinking he may have brain damage. I kept replaying the fall in my mind. I'm not sure if my reconstruction of it is accurate or not, but I see the cart stopping him a bit—

he scraped his chin where the cart opened—and I see his little hands up just enough to break his fall.

He didn't even have a lump. I gave him Tylenol. And awakened him two hours after he fell asleep. Now he's still his obnoxious, tyrannical four-year-old self. And I'm still having trouble sleeping nights, I keep seeing the fall.

Maybe I was so affected because my father almost died the previous week. He tried to get up in the night to go to the bathroom. Either he's tired of depending upon my mother to care for him or he awakens disoriented and has forgotten about the stroke. He falls again, breaking his hip. Seventy-four years old, in fragile health.

It's the drugs, the doctors and nurses say after my father's hip replacement surgery. Why my father is so far removed. It is the drugs, I think, yet I've seen that look before, that look of I'm not here too much longer. I saw it on my brother a few hours before he died. Heat waves took my paternal grandparents. Both had strokes. I get very frightened of head injury. I've seen too many young people on too many hospital rehab wards where my father has been, victims of overdoses, gunshot wounds, auto accidents, brain damaged all of them. Why I keep seeing my son's fall.

◆

I live near the University of Redlands. Sometimes famous people are brought in to speak on campus. Pat Riley spoke for convocation one year. At the height of the Lakers' winning seasons. Pat Riley arrived in a helicopter, which landed right on the quad. About a month ago Cindy

Crawford was on campus filming a t.v. commercial. I tried to get my four-year-old to go over to campus but he doesn't give a shit about Cindy Crawford. Unlike the future king of England. Once I heard Geraldine Ferraro speak at the chapel. Geraldine Ferraro, if you've forgotten, was the Democratic nominee for Vice President of the United States. She said she didn't hold it against Dan Quayle for not serving in Vietnam. He was in some sort of reserve capacity, I believe. Geraldine Ferraro said that any mother would have wanted to keep her child out of *that* war.

And now Robert McNamara, one of the principle strategists of the American involvement of the war in Vietnam, has said in his book that we had no objective in Vietnam, that we couldn't win, and that he knew all this but supported the war anyway. Robert McNamara, Secretary of Defense, an administrator, after all.

I think of all the souls who left this planet shrouded in the violence of that war and that geography and I think of myself and I think of those Marine officers who want housing by the water above Cotton's Point.

◆

My friend, poet and novelist Richard Means Ybarra, tile setter, and new member of the Chicano Surfing Association, was surfing a few weeks ago at Camp Pendleton. He went with his friends from Santa Cruz, a guy he went to UC Santa Cruz with, and his former doctor who surfs and is a retired captain in the military. The doctor, the retired captain, is able to use one of the mobile homes on the Marine base. The mobile homes are above Church, the surf break south of Lower Trestles.

After Ricardo and his friends surfed all day they began drinking beer with some of the Marines who themselves were staying in the mobile homes. They were enlisted men, Gulf War veterans. Probably getting a reward for hazardous duty, the way my father had those many years ago. On the beach below them other Marines were having a beer bust. They got very drunk, competing among themselves for the attention of the few women who were on the beach, Ricardo told me. They got into a fight. Ricardo said that he mentioned to the Marines he was drinking with, I thought Marines were supposed to be tough. Those guys fight like girls, Ricardo said. His comments were met with silence. And then laughter, for the Marines agreed. The guys fighting on the beach didn't much know how to fist fight.

♦

I broke a tooth the previous week. It needed a crown. They gave me Novocaine, at the dentist's office, but it didn't entirely numb my tooth. I said nothing to the dentist but she saw me flinching as she drilled my tooth. She gave me another shot then returned to complete the drilling. Still the tooth was not numb. I told the dentist to finish anyway.

At first I tensed and relaxed and sweated. I concentrated on the moment, on the pain, and the smell of my burning tooth. I couldn't take the pain, so I began doing *kata* in my mind. I worked the same one over and over. *Annanko*. One that I did over one hundred times in two days to instill it in my memory.

I can't say that I enjoyed the pain at any point, yet I was

one with it, enlightened almost, sort of like Kafka's protagonist in the story "The Penal Colony." Where they have the perfect torture machine.

My reasoning for enduring the pain of having my molar drilled went something like this: If Mahatma Gandhi could have gall bladder surgery with no anesthetic and while awake, I could certainly endure a little drilling after two shots of Novocain, even though the tooth wasn't numb.

◆

When I was an adolescent in the tenth grade in high school I went to a concert in the gymnasium at the new campus at UC Irvine. Janis Joplin and Big Brother and the Holding Company played, along with Buffalo Springfield. Everybody was taking drugs—dropping acid and smoking pot—and drinking alcohol. During Buffalo Springfield's set someone let loose a huge python snake, a snake that was longer than the wave is high that Juan Valdez and his burro surf. The snake moved through the crowd, over the dancers while the strobe lights flashed and the light-show pulsed.

I'm afraid of snakes.

And I kept my eye on that python, watching it slither over the crowd, happy revelers glad to help the snake on its journey.

As the snake worked its way back to where I stood, I left the gym. A friend and I walked out into the fields behind the gym, and we stood out in the moonlight. We didn't talk much, just enjoyed the quiet after the chaos of the rock concert. After we stood there for a time we realized that there were thousands of rabbits in the hills, bobbing around, doing their nocturnal rabbit dance.

I love the land of California. I loved being surrounded by all those rabbits that night. I decided then and there I would go to the university.

It wasn't that far from my home, maybe ten miles as the crow flies. I applied to UC Irvine as a senior in high school. I was turned down. I moved to Oregon, where I attended community college. I again applied to UC Irvine after completing my freshmen and sophomore course work. Again I was turned down. They said they wouldn't accept any of my coursework done at the Oregon community college. I finished my undergraduate coursework in Oregon, at Portland State University, and then set about finishing my education. I wanted to be able to build a house. I wanted to travel through Europe. After I accomplished those two elements of my education and after getting sidetracked a number of years making money, I decided to apply to UC Irvine's graduate program in writing. The one I mentioned earlier. Yet again I was turned down. By the school that is virtually in the backyard of my childhood home.

I called the English Department and got the office hours of the director of the program. I showed up unannounced during his office hours. Not to confront him but to ask how I might get accepted. The director told me that he didn't know whether or not his decisions were the right ones. I did find out, however, that I had been the sixth choice until a guy who had a novel out applied. Then I got bumped. I asked the director of the program why would a guy who's already publishing novels need to be in a writing program where they supposedly teach you to write a novel? He didn't have an answer for me.

At that time I was friends with a young woman who was an undergraduate at UC Irvine, a student of the director's. He got word to me through his student to apply to Squaw Valley, a summer writers workshop. The director told my friend to tell me there was a good chance I'd get a scholarship.

I applied the following year and did get a scholarship. I'd also been accepted with a scholarship into the writing program at the University of Washington, and accepted at the University of Arizona. I wanted to go to graduate school at Arizona because I'd already lived in the Northwest, and had never lived in the desert Southwest before.

And this: I got married. The first one.

When I met my wife I had a '61 Porsche, a three-quarter ton pickup truck, a small but thriving business, and money. And then we got married and I entered graduate school at U of A. Not what she signed on for, I see now in retrospect.

We had a huge wedding (I'd wanted a small one) and planned a honeymoon in Lake Tahoe so that I could attend the writers workshop before we moved to Arizona for my graduate studies. I know now the marriage was doomed when I let my wife fly home alone from our honeymoon, while I stayed on to attend a writers conference.

The conference would be good for my career, the director said.

And it was. At the conference I met a writer who would win a Pulitzer. He liked my writing and told me to apply to the program again. He was one of the first graduates of the program. And an editor with *Esquire* liked my short fiction as well, even taking back stories of mine to New York with him to show to an agent. The agent really loved my stuff, contacted me, and said, Send me a manuscript. She also encouraged me to send her whatever I wrote while in graduate school, and her kind praise helped me to withstand the batterings I took in the graduate school writing program.

I reapplied to UC Irvine, and the fourth time was the charm, I was accepted; the director of the program wrote me a nice letter—he was instrumental in my finally getting accepted at Irvine My first wife and I moved into the married student housing, which overlooks the very same field where I saw all those rabbits the night of the concert. But our marriage promptly ended. Right after our first anniversary, though it took some time to finalize the divorce. She couldn't handle the "student" life. And I don't blame her.

The next summer I spent in Baja California, preparing my manuscript to give to the agent. And talking to the people of Ensenada about the beggar women, and body surfing, and pining away over a failed marriage.

When I returned to school in the autumn, I met my *real* wife. She was a visiting writer and supervisor of teaching assistants. My supervisor. I asked her out toward the end of the first semester that we knew each other. On our first date we went to the movies. *Sid and Nancy*.

When I finished my thesis I sent it to the agent who'd encouraged me through graduate school. Send me a book-length manuscript, she'd told me. Except when I sent the book the agent was on maternity leave, and an assistant read the novel, and she didn't much care for it, and that was that. I sent my manuscript to three other agents, none of whom took it on. I gave up looking for an agent.

Five years later, after I'd finished my second novel, I

looked for an agent in earnest. I was turned down by over thirty of them. I'd given up sending it out when I spoke with an editor who was including a short piece of mine in an anthology he was compiling. He told me to try an editor at a large publishing house. The editor was looking for Chicano fiction, this editor told me. I spoke with the editor only to find out that he was looking for nonfiction. He did, however, kindly tell me to send him my novel. I did. I never heard back from him so I called. He'd obviously read the opening, had liked it, but told me to give more time.

My phone calls became a joke with us. Every month or two I'd give him a call, he'd refer to the opening of the novel, and tell me he liked it. I knew this, he would never read the entire manuscript. Finally, about ten months later, the editor suggested two agents who were interested in Latino issues. One of the agents had already turned me down. I tried the other agent and was taken on! I was very pleased, I had a New York literary agent.

I was in communication with the agent's assistants, periodically checking to make sure they were sending out my novel. They did sent it out to three places right away, and received three quick rejections. They stopped sending it out. It took me over a year to discern this fact. Part of the problem was that the assistants kept leaving, and I didn't have access to the agent, ergo I had to keep establishing relationships with assistants.

In the meantime I finished another novel. This time I decided to go to New York to meet with the agent. I did so, handing her my new manuscript. Told her to let me know right away whether or not she wished to handle this novel. I was moving on, if she didn't respond quickly. I must say, however, that I really liked my agent, and we hit it off. But just in case, I met another agent while in NYC. A young agent, an agent who was hot. An agent who represents writers who sell their manuscripts for a million dollars, as did one of the guys I was in graduate school with, or so the rumor goes. The young, hot agent loved my book. Had no idea where to sell it. If I were younger or sexier, the young agent said, she might be able to place the book.

I called my agent a number of times but could not speak with her. I told all this to Ricardo. He prodded me to try his agent, but I resisted because it was inculcated in me that you were supposed to have a New York agent, if you're a serious writer.

Finally, I showed my novel to Ricardo's agent. She liked the book. Said she'd work hard to sell it. But she's on the West Coast, I kept thinking. Yet the advice given to me by an art critic friend resonated in my mind: Go where you're wanted.

New York doesn't give a shit about me. Doesn't give a shit about Latino issues or brown people or California, unless it's some form of exotic or strange behavior. Doesn't give a shit about the Chicano Surfing Association. Go where you're wanted.

I went to Ricardo's agent's house. She and her husband, a well-known philosopher, were getting ready to leave the country for a philosophy convention, and there were a bunch of writers at Ricardo's agent's house, trying to tie up loose ends before she left. It felt wonderful being there, a real literary environment, a place where artists and thinkers met. I was hooked.

I often tell my students that if you plan on making

185

money with your writing, you'd be better off getting a job at McDonald's. The work would be steadier, less frustrating, and you'd almost certainly make more money.

I don't write to make money.

I write because my mother was unable to hold me until four days after my birth—seems I'd lost oxygen and the nurses wouldn't let my mother see me; they thought I was too dark. My mother told me on my last birthday, when I visited her and my invalid father. The nurses thought that she would think I was too dark.

I write because I was the second child, and wanted someone to hear my voice.

I write because I'm part of the second minority group in the United States.

I write because I love to write.

And this: I don't know why it is I have this urge to sit down every day and communicate through the typewriter. Some of the above is part of it. It's as good an endeavor as building houses, or printing, or surfing, or picking coffee beans, I suppose. It's something to do. Something to pass the time.

What I've learned:

This place where we're all entrenched in the dramas of our daily lives is called Earth. It's a planet in a Solar System of the Milky Way. One of billions of planets. One solar system among billions. It's not called heaven, it's not called hell. It's Earth and there are things we're supposed to learn.

To hold your breath longer, exhale.

Termites eat the dead wood.

You have to eat in order to lose weight.

Bricks are stronger apart, thus the mortar.

Action precedes motivation.

♦

Oh, look! my mother said. I was driving. We were coming back from the hospital, where we'd visited my father. We had turned onto a street that was completely canopied by purple-blooming jacaranda trees.

♦

Look! my son said. It had rained for a brief time and raindrops were setup because of the cold and they hugged the clover petals that ringed our lawn, each drop reflecting the now bright sunlight.

♦

I went to visit my friend Ricardo yesterday. He lives at Paradise Cove in Malibu. We walked through a cove down to the ocean, where the surf was rising. The swell was up, building steadily, and the tide was falling, a great time for surfers. There was excitement everywhere, the waves large and long in the dusky summer mist.

Ricardo wore his Chicano Surfing Association T-shirt. The shirt's in big demand there among older surfers. A number of guys want them. One guy told me that he really was part Chicano. Later I told Ricardo that his friend should get one. Ricardo told me that the guy wasn't a writer, therefore he couldn't get a T-shirt.

I was introduced to all of Ricardo's surfing buddies as

the president of the Chicano Surfing Association. It sounded special, desirable.

Did you tell them it's a writers club? I said to Ricardo.

I didn't bother, Ricardo said.

♦

Oftentimes I think of Pilate's last utterance at the end of Toni Morrison's magnificent novel *Song of Solomon*. Pilate's about to die, just before Milkman flies, and Pilate says, I wish I'd a knowed more people. I would've loved 'em all. If I'd a knowed more, I would a loved more. I think about that line, a lot.

And I wish I weren't ambivalent about the Marine officer's housing above Cotton's Point.

My *sensei* says that we are a ten percent society. By this he means that we only concentrate on the worst 10% of our lives, ignoring the other benevolent or pleasurable 90%. He's on to something here. My *sensei* is. On to something.

MEDITATION

I've read that, on average, males spend one-half hour per day with their children. On average, world wide. I'm pretty smug about this detail. During the school year when my wife and I teach, I spend an average of over thirty hours a week with my son. I think I'm a good parent, and an excellent caregiver.

Our son has only been baby-sat twice in his life. This was a decision on my wife's and my part. We would take up the slack, which mostly fell on my wife. I can see the biological setup clearly: mother nurturing and unlimited love; father nurturing too, but there's a difference. A physical boundary the young male learns with his father, something he doesn't quite perceive with his mother. These kinds of observations have taught me much about the life biology class in session at our house. Men aren't women. Men don't lactate, don't carry the child to term in their bodies, aren't biologically equipped to do so. Similarly, women are not men. My wife doesn't wrestle with my son. Some mothers may like to wrestle with their sons, I don't know. I love wrestling hard with my son. He's like a bear cub, learning the moves.

The reason I mention all of the above is that on my watch, my son was jumping and fell and cracked his head on the hearth. On the last day of July.

This summer was trying. As mentioned earlier, my father fell while trying to get out of bed by himself in the middle of the night. He had to have hip replacement surgery. In July my mother had a surgical procedure. Even my dog had three surgeries to finally remove a foxtail that had become embedded in her abdomen. After I brought my dog home from the vet the last time, I thought the worst might be over, thought I'd weathered the storm. After major health shit for my father, mother, and even my dog, I thought I'd be let off the hook.

Not so. My son had thirteen stitches in his forehead. Three underneath, ten on the surface. You could see his little skull. On my watch.

The day prior, my son and I had gone to Walmart to buy a couch bed that my mother might be able to sleep on, should she spend the night, which she's only done once. We thought it would be a nice touch. Something always here for her. But my son saw a child's couch bed, one with dinosaurs on it, and fell in love with it so I bought it for him. He couldn't stay away from the thing, jumping all over it, hiding inside of it, moving it from place to place. He loved that couch. Truly loved it.

While I was feeding him pizza he placed it next to the leather couch, our regular couch. We have a game in which he walks around and snatches bits of pizza when he gets close. He had just snatched a bite. He climbed onto the leather couch, jumped down on his couch, jumped again, hit a high spot where the dinosaur couch turns into a bed, and launched himself toward the hearth. He put his hands out and broke his fall, but the hearth is slightly raised in relation to the carpet, and this is where, I think, the accident occurred. He misjudged the height of the hearth for he's had no experience with it. And his forehead smacked the hearthstones.

I watched it. Unable to respond until after the action ceased. I scooped him into my arms and held him to me and felt the blood drops on my shoulder. He was crying the "real," the hurt cry. I took him into the bathroom and put a damp washcloth on his forehead, putting pressure on the cut. I yelled to my wife, who was just starting a nap. She took over so I could call the doctor. We have an HMO and I wasn't sure what we were supposed to do in an emergency. If it's life threatening, I know you call 911. This was bloody, but not life-in-danger stuff, I didn't think.

The receptionist put me on hold.

Then a nurse came on and told me I had to take my son to the extended care facility in Highland. I'd have to get on a freeway. A new one. I didn't know how to catch the freeway. The nurse couldn't tell me. The previous extended care place was probably two minutes away by car. The nurse reassured me that the new place was less than ten minutes from my house. Once I got on the freeway, which I, and nobody else, seemed to know how to do. I became impatient and told the nurse I was taking my son to the Redland's Hospital emergency room, about one minute from my house. The nurse told me she'd try to get the doctor's authorization for this. She put me on hold. For a long time.

I took ice to my wife and she placed it directly over our son's gash. It was wide but the blood flow had almost ceased.

The nurse came back on the line; she told me the doctor would not authorize an ER room visit. Our provider had the capability to stitch wounds at the Highlands facility, the nurse told me. I was probably on the phone twelve minutes. I lost it, especially when nobody could tell me how to get to the new facility.

We did make it to the extended care facility in less than ten minutes—I was driving 85 miles per hour. The doctor was good. He calmed my son, who thought he was going to die. He soothed my son, explaining everything to him. The doctor stuck a large needle into the wound three, four, five times, while my wife and I held him. He cried but remained still. When the wound was anesthetized my son became less agitated. The doctor put three metal stitches under the surface, as I've said, and ten visible.

After the stitching, my son thanked the doctor, told him he'd done a good job, was a fine doctor. Four-years old.

On the way home we stopped at The World of Discovery store. I bought my son a bunch of toy animals, which he has a profound and deep love for.

For the next two weeks, as a coping mechanism, my son built an assemblage in the living room that he called Jurassic Wild. And for that time, he got out every toy he owns, and he owns an incredible amount, a truly incredible amount, and he created scenes in boxes, little dioramas. He covered the boxes with stickers and we made numerous trips to toy stores to accommodate his artistic vision. His creation took over the living room and dining room. It was summer, he couldn't go out in the sun.

And now I know how Picasso's father must have felt. When he gave the juvenile Picasso all his painting equipment, for the son was far beyond the father. I always interpreted Picasso's father's action as one of defeat, one of bitterness possibly. Now I think it was probably a joyous gift. A liberation. The son so far evolved. The four-year-old child as inspiration.

♦

Half of the stitches were removed yesterday morning. The doctor said the three underneath the skin would remain there. He will have a scar but we've been putting aloe vera on it, and when the stitches are all out we'll switch to vitamin E. My aunt told me the remedy my grandmother used was called Concha Nacar. I have a great aunt named Concha, who's in her nineties, and I couldn't resist the pun, Concha's *nalgas*. My aunt said she'd get some. The doctor said no sunlight on the cut for three months. To use vitamin E for one year. And the stitches will remain in his head.

On my watch.

He's four, I'm the adult. I should have stopped him from jumping, especially while eating. There seem to be two schools of thought about the accident. They're generational. The older generation is of the attitude that kids will do what they'll do regardless of how close you watch them. The younger generation thinks that yes, it was your responsibility, but don't beat yourself up over it.

Thus far the gash is about three inches long. But it's been less than a week and it's coming together nicely. Some people say that the skin on the forehead grows back onto the scalp so the scar will disappear. The doctor said this is not the case. Others say, well, he'll grow up with the scar, will get used to it, and it won't be a big thing. One person said hard-headed people have to get hit a few times. My son said that he'd wanted to get it over with.

In martial arts there's a state called perfect awareness. The well-developed martial artist exhibits this quality of being aware of everything at once. He will never be in a confrontation because he will spot it in advance, thereby avoiding it. I don't know how many times I've caught my son in mid-fall, thus preventing injury. Since there's no injury, you don't remember the incident.

And here's my problem: I wasn't aware, three times. I hit him with the closet door. When my wife visited her mother I let my son get in a shopping cart and fall on his head. I let my son jump close to the hearth, which he hit. Bashed in the head three times.

This is not awareness, even though I spend over thirty hours a week with him.

◆

Last week I visited my father. He's now in a convalescent hospital. My mother wasn't strong enough to care for him when he came home from the hospital from his hip replacement surgery. He wasn't strong enough to help her with the transfers from the wheelchair to the bed, to the toilet, to the couch. My mother was still recovering from her surgery. When I arrived at the hospital my father wasn't in his room. I inquired about him, and was sent down to the therapy room in the basement. My father was lying on a large bench, a therapist massaging his paralyzed leg. He had raved about this therapist on my previous visit so I was glad to get a chance to meet him. To thank him for helping my father.

Another woman was using the parallel bars that were attached to a ramp. Where my father would stand up. I've seen him stand up before, even helped him do so at his home in front of the sink where it's wide and sturdy. I assumed he'd stand up and sit back down, all in a few seconds. When the woman was finished using the parallel bars, my father kept pointing to them. We tried to figure out what he was telling us. There was a cloth on the bar; the other therapist removed it. My father persisted, continuing to point to a place by the ramp's entrance. Finally, one of the therapists noticed the puddle of liquid my father pointed to. He had always been fastidious.

After the urine was cleaned from the ramp, my father got his turn. The therapist told me I could help by controlling the wheelchair.

The therapist stood my father, sat before him on a rolling stool, and prodded my father. My father threw his good leg forward, followed it by dragging his paralyzed leg behind him. A step. My father was walking!

My vision of my father has changed in the last four years. He's going to be seventy-six years old, and for seventy-two of those years he was ambulatory. I sometimes forget that all the years I knew him, he was mobile. And now he'd worked so hard to become "mobile" once again.

When I took him back to his room I told him how proud I was of him, to see him walk. I put my arm around my father a lot because it seems to me that the old and infirm no longer get human touch other than by paid strangers. I had a manila folder with me. In it were the title pages to this manuscript. Time was moving forward; I wanted to show him what I was working on. He read the prologue and became teary eyed. My father did.

I told him the book was for him. For all the things he'd shown me and taught me and given me. After he got control of his emotions he asked me, What about your mother?

◆

The morning we took my son to get part of his stitches out we were going to go to IHOP (catchy, sexy title that) to have breakfast. The doctor removed my son's bandage, removed every other stitch, and then put on the equivalent of butterfly bandages over the wound. Most of the cut wasn't showing. But my son hadn't seen it with the stitches out. He'd seen it at home when we changed bandages. While we drove to get breakfast he asked his mother for a mirror. She handed him a compact from her purse. He looked at himself in silence while I drove. After a time he said, How about we go home?

We asked him if he felt badly about his cut. He said no, he didn't feel badly about it. It might make people sad when they see it, he said.

◆

Last night at karate training we worked on a *kata* called *Unsu*. Cloud hands. It begins very gently. Then it moves quickly in four different directions. One falls to the ground and kicks while on the ground. Then one disarms an opponent, followed by a series of highly complex moves, twists and kicks and body torques while on one leg. I love the

196

kata. I'm not very good at it, however. Following training, while in the line up, our *sensei* said that the *kata* is about a sudden, fierce storm. He went on to say that no storm lasts more than one hundred days.

◆

Tomorrow morning the rest of my son's stitches will be removed. He says that this time he will go out for breakfast after. My wife and I have agreed that we will cover his cut with a band-aid. We're lucky in that regard. My son has a band-aid fetish, covering his skin even if there's no cut. My wife says that this is because of his aversion to imperfection.

My father is once again coming home from the hospital. I'm on call to bring him home. Oftentimes they don't give us much warning. An administrator will decide that the insurance coverage is over, and bam, he's released. So I'm on watch. And I'm taking my son to get his stitches removed tomorrow. The way things are going, probably both will happen the same day. If they do, then it will be a good day indeed.

◆

My father did return home after his hip replacement surgery. It wasn't on the same day my son had his stitches removed. It was a considerable time later; he had to remain in the convalescent hospital until he was strong enough to help my mother with his transfers.

My son's scar is healing nicely. You won't even notice it

in a year, his pediatrician said when I took my son in for an ear infection.

My son's stitches were removed on a Wednesday. A number of weeks later I brought my father home. It was a Friday. The next Friday we went on our vacation, my wife, my son, and me. To the Hotel del Coronado. On Coronado Island in San Diego. A break from routine. Usually we stay at Moonlight Beach, in a motel, for a week. But when I'd made the reservations back in spring, I didn't realize that our vacation coincided with the Republican National Convention to be held in San Diego. Moonlight Beach is just south of Encinitas. Not exactly Republican country, my wife said. I refused to be that near that many Republicans—too many evil vibes with all those fatuous politicians in the area.

So we changed our routine, going for fewer days at a nicer place, and during a different week, a week when no politicians would inundate the sunny confines of San Diego. My son and I had never stayed in an elegant hotel before. I didn't know what a key card was. By the end of the first day my son was insisting that he open the door to our room. So that he could see the green light go on in the door lock when it opened.

The ocean was cold, though the air was hot, and we had a lovely time. We'd put a band-aid over the healing cut, and my son wore a baseball cap except when he and I were in the surf. After spending a good chunk of the day on the beach the three of us would wander about the hotel's grounds, eating in a terrace restaurant that overlooks the Pacific. Or my wife and I would drink margaritas by the pool in the late afternoon while our son still wished to play in the water. It was idyllic. It was a vacation.

There was one big problem, however. The Hotel del Coronado has a faux art gallery in one of the entry halls. Among all the touristy prints and photos was a Leroy Neiman print. My son hates Leroy Neiman paintings. Four-years old and has a tremendous negative response to the Neiman aesthetic. He goes to the library and "rents," his term, Georgia O'Keeffe prints, which he hangs at his eye level, and studies. Studies them for long periods. We'd had a dicey afternoon once when in Seal Beach after frolicking in the summer surf all day we'd stopped at a Burger King to get our child a kid's meal. The Burger King had a Leroy Neiman print on the wall. My son couldn't stop looking at it. And complaining. He wouldn't even eat. After being at the beach all day. We finally had to make him switch seats so he couldn't see the print, but, still, he kept craning his neck so he could complain. Reminded me of his namesake, another opinionated art critic.

So when we walked into one of the lobbies my son bellowed out, Oh no! Not Leroy Neiman! This brought appreciative laughter from a few other guests. The further problem was that my son wanted to check out of the hotel. Didn't wish to remain in a place that would hang a Leroy Neiman print. He wanted to go to the other, cheaper motel. We bribed him with toys from the hotel's toy store, and told ourselves to steer clear of that particular lobby.

Our last day of vacation—it was a three night, four day stay—was bittersweet, to say the least. We'd had a few days of ocean sun, and lived as if we had money, every need covered by credit cards. The next day I'd start teaching again. After nine months off for sabbatical. One day on the beach drinking margaritas, the next day trying to teach college in a trailer with air conditioning, which if it works you can't hear, and if it doesn't work you can't think. The School of Humanities where I teach is the only school still teaching in trailers post Northridge earthquake. One student told me she was sorry I was back, I seemed in such a bad mood. And I was; I'd have to snap out of it.

I called my mother to give her our vacation update. I'd talked to her a few times while we were at the Hotel del Coronado, but I wanted to keep in touch to see what was going on with my father. She went into a litany of my father's problems, but from what I could make out, it sounded as if he had the flu. He didn't. He was truly ill. Turned out he had a "red hot" gall bladder and needed it removed. Except that all his organs were shutting down, and he had a fever, and they wouldn't operate on him until he was no longer dehydrated. The operation was further complicated by all his other problems: history of heart attack, open heart surgery, stroke, brain seizure, still healing from hip replacement surgery six weeks prior. And Labor Day Weekend was approaching. He was admitted on Wednesday. I saw him on Thursday. The previous Friday I'd brought him home. And then gone on vacation.

The doctor said they'd operate on Saturday or Tuesday. I found that interesting since Labor Day fell on Monday. Gee, they'd operate before or after the holiday. My father wasn't strong enough for the operation on Saturday. So Tuesday it was. His temperature shot up on Sunday, and after his surgery a nurse told us that his gall bladder had burst. The surgeon neglected to tell us this minor detail.

The pain I saw my father suffer that week should not be

endured by any living person. My father was on a morphine "push," which meant that every three hours a nurse
would put morphine into his IV tube. And still, he was in
terrible pain. And this: he had the hiccups. For over a week.
And every time he hiccuped he had excruciating pain in his
torso. The pain he endured made me think of the Crucifix-
ion. Jesus died to show us how much pain we would suffer. Good karma is dying in your sleep. Or dying the first
day of the stroke.

I watched my father suffer that week, suffer as no person
should.

But he survived still another time. The doctors kept him
alive.

And he went into a convalescent hospital once more.
Again, my mother told him she'd bring him home. I want
to bring him home one more time, my mother said. He'd
not been home a week before his gall bladder crisis. She
wanted him to enjoy the comfort of his own surroundings.
Wanted him to die peacefully at home.

My father had not eaten solid food for weeks, was very
feeble. When I lifted him onto the wheelchair the day my
mother and I brought him home, he was so light, nothing
like the man who'd taught me the ways of the world.

Still, it was a very special day. My father was coming
home once again. And I was reading an essay that night at
Barnes & Noble in Northridge. Many of my students were
there, and they knew my father was very ill because I'd
missed class when we thought he would die, and I told
them how glad I was to read on this day of all days since I
was reading an essay in an anthology, an essay I'd written
about my father—"Of Cholos and Surfers." The day I

brought him home, I told my students. They were optimistic, saying things like, He'll get better, now that he's home. I couldn't tell them that the reason my father was home was so that he might die in comfortable surroundings. That day I'd driven from Redlands to Huntington Beach, sixty miles, brought my father home, drove from Huntington Beach to Northridge, forty miles, read, and then drove home to Redlands, ninety miles. My father was home, it was a good day.

♦

I've been training karate every Monday and Wednesday night for six years. I never visit my parents on Wednesday night. I train. But something was calling me to my father. My intuition was talking, and I listened. I knew I was going to see him that Wednesday night, just five days after I'd brought him home.

When I got to my parent's house, my father was in severe pain. My mother and I took him to the hospital ER. It takes five hours to run the checks and get him admitted, my mother said. She knew the drill. We got to the hospital at 7:30 p.m. My father was in his own room and on a diluadid "push" by 12:30 a.m. Five hours.

The emergency room doctor had looked vaguely familiar to me. It wasn't until I saw her move quickly—a young man was coming in with a stroke, she thought he might be a "bleeder," I heard her say on the phone as she ordered personnel and equipment to the ER—that I recognized her. It was because when she ran, she had an odd gait. She was pigeon-toed, but this coupled with the fact that she wore clogs made her have a truly unique run. I'd seen her flat out sprint four-and-half years ago when she saved my father's life. Code Blue. Sprinting from ER to intensive care, where my father was.

While we were in the ER my father kept apologizing to my mother and me. For having to bring him. For having to stay up so late. I don't know why I was called to visit my father on a Wednesday night. I know why I was visiting my father on a Wednesday night. My mother couldn't load him into the car. The ER nurse had trouble putting him on the gurney—I could move him easily without hurting him. I could help the x-ray technician manipulate and hold my father in positions he couldn't get into or hold himself. Why I was called.

The hospital is a lonely place at night, and you feel vulnerable, my mother said. She too thanked me for being with her. It was a little after one in the morning when I got her home.

On my drive home I heard on the news that once again motorists were attacked by vandals that night. There were all sorts of theories as to who and with what the rear windows of cars on the freeway were being blasted out. Seventeen more that night. Two hundred in the past few days. Ice cubes. Marbles. Bakelight, the stuff that spark plugs are made out of. Even a high-pitched new weapon that humans can't hear, being tested by government agents. Some of the many theories.

Last week I'd been diverted off the freeway late at night returning from teaching my night class. A woman had taken a cabbie hostage. In Palm Springs. The cab ran out of gas on the San Bernardino Freeway. And there the standoff remained. The SWAT team around the cab. The woman inside with the cabbie. All us motorists forced into one lane, and then taken off the freeway, surrounded by those late-night trucks that look like the sides of canyons.

The radio also told me that the freeway I was on would close to one lane. Due to "police activity." This didn't much concern me for there was very little traffic. It was almost two in the morning. It wasn't much of a delay, in fact it was no delay at all, as I suspected.

A bunch of Highway Patrol cars blocked the freeway down to one lane, as the radio had said. And there were spotlights set up on the freeway. And there was a body on the ground. Covered with a yellow tarp. Awash in white light.